DATE DUE

COMPACT *Research*

Phobias

by Hal Marcovitz

Diseases and Disorders

ReferencePoint
Press™

San Diego, CA

For more information, contact:
ReferencePoint Press, Inc.
PO Box 27779
San Diego, CA 92198
www.ReferencePointPress.com

Picture credits:
Maury Aaseng: 33–35, 50–53, 69–73, 89–92
AP Images: 11
iStockphoto.com: 15

LIBRARY OF CONGRESS CATALOGING-IN-PUBLICATION DATA

Marcovitz, Hal.
   Phobias / by Hal Marcovitz.
      p. cm. — (Compact research)
   Includes bibliographical references and index.
   ISBN-13: 978-1-60152-044-9 (hardback)
   ISBN-10: 1-60152-044-1 (hardback)
   1. Phobias. I. Title.
   RC535.M368 2008
   616.85'225—dc22
                                                                                    2008010894

Contents

Foreword   4

Phobias at a Glance   6

Overview   8

What Are Phobias?   19
    Primary Source Quotes   27
    Facts and Illustrations   32

What Causes Phobias?   37
    Primary Source Quotes   44
    Facts and Illustrations   49

How Do Phobias Affect People?   55
    Primary Source Quotes   63
    Facts and Illustrations   68

Can People Overcome Phobias?   75
    Primary Source Quotes   83
    Facts and Illustrations   88

Key People and Advocacy Groups   94

Chronology   96

Related Organizations   98

For Further Research   102

Source Notes   105

List of Illustrations   107

Index   108

About the Author   112

Foreword

As modern civilization continues to evolve, its ability to create, store, distribute, and access information expands exponentially. The explosion of information from all media continues to increase at a phenomenal rate. By 2020 some experts predict the worldwide information base will double every 73 days. While access to diverse sources of information and perspectives is paramount to any democratic society, information alone cannot help people gain knowledge and understanding. Information must be organized and presented clearly and succinctly in order to be understood. The challenge in the digital age becomes not the creation of information, but how best to sort, organize, enhance, and present information.

ReferencePoint Press developed the *Compact Research* series with this challenge of the information age in mind. More than any other subject area today, researching current issues can yield vast, diverse, and unqualified information that can be intimidating and overwhelming for even the most advanced and motivated researcher. The *Compact Research* series offers a compact, relevant, intelligent, and conveniently organized collection of information covering a variety of current topics ranging from illegal immigration and methamphetamine to diseases such as anorexia and meningitis.

The series focuses on three types of information: objective single-author narratives, opinion-based primary source quotations, and facts and statistics. The clearly written objective narratives provide context and reliable background information. Primary source quotes are carefully selected and cited, exposing the reader to differing points of view. And facts and statistics sections aid the reader in evaluating perspectives. Presenting these key types of information creates a richer, more balanced learning experience.

For better understanding and convenience, the series enhances information by organizing it into narrower topics and adding design features that make it easy for a reader to identify desired content. For example, in *Compact Research: Illegal Immigration*, a chapter covering the economic impact of illegal immigration has an objective narrative explaining the various ways the economy is impacted, a balanced section of numerous primary source quotes on the topic, followed by facts and full-color illustrations to encourage evaluation of contrasting perspectives.

The ancient Roman philosopher Lucius Annaeus Seneca wrote, "It is quality rather than quantity that matters." More than just a collection of content, the *Compact Research* series is simply committed to creating, finding, organizing, and presenting the most relevant and appropriate amount of information on a current topic in a user-friendly style that invites, intrigues, and fosters understanding.

Phobias at a Glance

What Is a Phobia?

A phobia is an anxiety disorder—an irrational worry about a normal, everyday event. Other anxiety disorders are panic disorder, obsessive-compulsive disorder, post-traumatic stress disorder, and generalized anxiety disorder.

Two Types of Phobias

Phobias fall into two general categories: specific and social. Social phobia is overwhelming anxiety and excessive self-consciousness about everyday social situations. Specific phobias are intense and irrational fears about otherwise harmless things such as spiders, airplane flight, or elevators.

Who Is Phobic?

Some 15 million Americans suffer from social phobia while 19 million harbor specific phobias; women and men are afflicted with social phobia in equal numbers, but women are more likely to harbor specific phobias, probably due to pressures placed on them by society as well as hormonal imbalances. Most phobias manifest themselves in childhood.

What Causes Phobias?

Mental health professionals suspect many causes, including frightening experiences in childhood, imbalances in the brain chemicals known as neurotransmitters, an overactive component of the brain known as the amygdala, and fears inherited from ancestors.

Main Symptoms

Social phobia sufferers avoid contact with other people or situations they find frightening, such as social gatherings or school events. People who harbor specific phobias avoid what they fear; they may decline to travel by airplane or avoid crossing bridges.

Further Complications

When confronted by what frightens them, phobia sufferers may lapse into a panic attack. During a panic attack they may experience pounding heart, perspiration, weakness, faintness, dizziness, chills, numbness, and chest pain, as well as feelings of unreality and impending doom.

Severe Consequences

People who suffer from social phobia may spend lifetimes in loneliness and isolation and fall into more severe mental illnesses, such as depression. People who harbor blood-injection-injury phobias may avoid seeking medical attention for possibly life-threatening illnesses.

Treatment

Most people who harbor phobias respond well to cognitive-behavioral therapy, which introduces them to small doses of what frightens them so that they can gradually overcome their fears. Antidepressant drugs are also effective.

Research Continues

Scientists are looking closely at the amygdala and whether drug therapy can alter its reaction to fearful situations. Therapists are also making wider use of virtual reality as a method of providing cognitive-behavioral therapy.

Overview

> **❝Were I now to unfold for you a scroll upon which I had written my phobias, it might stretch all the way to China.❞**
>
> —Allen Shawn, *Wish I Could Be There: Notes from a Phobic Life*.

Phobias are irrational and persistent fears that can be triggered by all manner of sources, including objects, situations, people, or activities. People who suffer from phobias attempt to avoid what causes their fears. If they fail and find themselves confronting what they fear, they may undergo intense psychological and physical reactions that could culminate in panic attacks.

Phobias are among a group of mental ills known as anxiety disorders. According to the National Institute of Mental Health, some 40 million Americans suffer from anxiety disorders. Generally, an anxiety disorder is an irrational worry about a normal, everyday event. An anxiety disorder can manifest itself in several forms, including phobias. Among the other types of anxiety disorders are panic disorder, in which an overwhelming sense of terror dominates an individual; obsessive-compulsive disorder, in which a person may develop a ridiculous ritual to deal with a fear, such as repeated washing of hands in response to a fear of germs; and post-traumatic stress disorder, in which a person's unpleasant memory may suddenly spark a reaction of terror.

While everybody experiences anxious moments, most people are able to confront their fears and develop rational responses. People who suffer from anxiety disorders have let their fears escalate to the point where they can no longer control their reactions to them. By letting their fears control their lives, people who suffer from anxiety disorders often find themselves in an endless spiral of terror and loneliness that can grow worse as time goes by. Says Richard Restak, professor of neurology at George Washington University Medical Center in Washington, D.C., and author of the book *Poe's Heart and the Mountain Climber: Exploring the Effect of Anxiety on Our Brains and Our Culture,*

> Anxiety tends to be a cumulative emotion: If we become anxious about something today, then our anxiety will re-surface whenever we encounter that same event or situation in the future. And since each day provides any number of anxiety-provoking events, the triggers for anxiety arousal increase over the years.[1]

Social Phobias

Generally, phobias are classified as either social phobia or specific phobias. People who suffer from social phobia are overwhelmingly anxious and excessively self-conscious in everyday social situations. They believe they are constantly watched and judged by others. They are in constant fear of embarrassing themselves in front of others.

From time to time, many people may harbor such fears. Anyone who has ever had to take the stage for the first time in a high school play or perform a solo in the annual band concert

> " By letting their fears control their lives, people who suffer from anxiety disorders often find themselves in an endless spiral of terror and loneliness that can grow worse as time goes by. "

is likely to suffer some degree of stage fright. But an ordinary case of stage fright and a social phobia are vastly different. Somebody who suffers from stage fright may feel nervous for a few minutes prior to taking the stage, but once he or she starts performing, those temporary pangs of nervousness usually pass. People who suffer from social phobia may spend days or even weeks worrying about upcoming events. Their fears will become so intense that they will interfere with their lives—affecting their school work, home life, and other activities. And when they attend the dreaded events, they will be intensely uncomfortable and worry for hours or even days afterward how they were judged by others. Of course, people who suffer from social phobia may not even go through with these events. They may find ways to avoid these experiences, calling in sick or making up excuses for why they cannot present their projects in front of their classes or go to school dances with their friends. According to the National Institute of Mental Health, as many as 15 million Americans suffer from some degree of social phobia.

Specific Phobias

A specific phobia is an intense and irrational fear of something that poses little or no threat, such as heights, escalators, tunnels, closed-in places, water, and flying. In most cases, people have their first experience with a specific phobia in childhood; the memory of a bad experience stays with them as they grow into adults and develops into a phobia. Perhaps as children they were frightened by a spider. Now they suffer from arachnophobia—fear of spiders.

> People who suffer from social phobia are overwhelmingly anxious and excessively self-conscious in everyday social situations.

The word *phobia* stems from the name Phobos, the ancient Greek god of fright. As such, most phobia names are drawn from the Greek words for the sources of the fears. *Arachni* is the Greek word for spider; hence, arachnophobia. Latin or English words provide the names for other phobias.

Unlike social phobia, specific phobias often do not dominate the lives of people who suffer from them. In most cases, people who harbor specific phobias are well aware of what frightens them, and they make special efforts to avoid their fears. That way, they can avoid the panic attacks or other consequences of confronting their fears. Sometimes, they can avoid what they fear with very little effort—if they are frightened of dogs, for example, they simply stay away from them.

However, that does not mean specific phobias do not have ways of impacting people's lives. Somebody who is afraid of crossing bridges may drive miles out of his or her way to avoid doing so. Somebody with a fear of elevators may turn down a job offer because the company's office is on

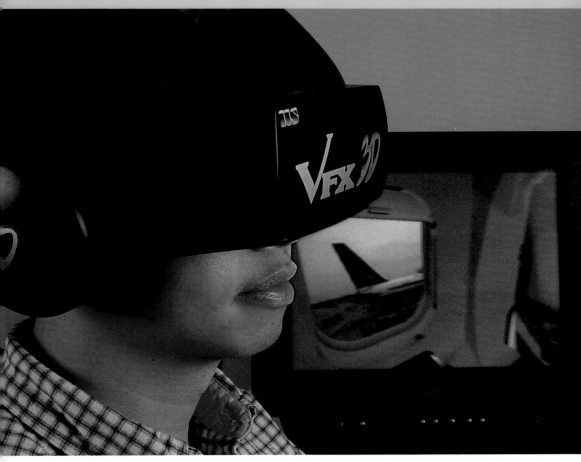

This researcher experiences a simulated airplane flight. Therapists are making wider use of virtual reality as a method of providing cognitive-behavioral therapy. Using equipment that can simulate fearful situations through the technique known as virtual reality, patients can receive in their doctors' offices prescribed doses of what frightens them. The therapists can use computers to control the experiences, giving their patients a taste of their fears.

the tenth floor. A picnic can be ruined if a spider suddenly walks across the picnic table where an arachnophobe is eating. It is believed that some 19 million Americans suffer from specific phobias.

What Causes Phobias?

Any situation involving other people can spark a reaction in someone who suffers from social phobia. Indeed, a person suffering from social phobia can experience a panic attack at a party, dinner, or school event.

For some people who harbor severe degrees of social phobia, just walking out the door may be too much to bear. Unless they can find a way to overcome their fears, they face a lifetime of isolation and loneliness.

> **A specific phobia is an intense and irrational fear of something that poses little or no threat, such as heights, escalators, tunnels, closed-in places, water, and flying.**

As for specific phobias, they can be as common as electrophobia, the fear of electricity that manifests itself when a person is afraid to plug in an electrical appliance. A person with ophidiophobia, a fear of snakes, cannot tolerate the sight of snakes, even to the point where he or she cannot bear to look at a picture of a snake in a textbook. Some people suffer from multiple phobias. Says Allen Shawn, author of the book *Wish I Could Be There: Notes from a Phobic Life*:

I don't like heights. I don't like being on the water. I am upset by walking across parking lots or open parks or fields where there are no buildings. I tend to avoid bridges, unless they are on a small scale. I respond poorly to stretches of vastness but do equally badly when I am closed in, as I am severely claustrophobic. When I go to a theater, I sit on the aisle. I am petrified of tunnels, making most train travel as well as many drives difficult. I don't take subways. I avoid elevators as much as possible. I experience glassed-in spaces as toxic, and I find it very difficult to adjust to being in buildings in which the windows don't open.[2]

Hundreds of causes for specific phobias are known. In fact, new phobias are constantly being discovered; they are often prompted by the changing social environment of life in America and elsewhere. For example, in the years before personal computers were a large part of everyone's lives, few people feared them. Now, with computers sitting atop desktops nearly everywhere in American society, the fear of computers, or cyberphobia, has become real and genuine in the lives of many people.

Physiological Explanations

The knowledge that many social and specific phobias are the result of trauma at a very early age has long been established. Still, a young child's bad memories of being lost at the mall or chased by an angry swarm of bees may not be the only cause of his or her phobias. Although phobias manifest themselves in emotional reactions, they may occur for physiological reasons.

Abnormalities in parts of the brain may be at the root of phobias. The amygdalae are two tiny, almond-shaped balls of tissue found near the center of the brain. The amygdalae control human emotions, including fear. When a situation prompts a fearful response in a person, the amygdalae activate a number of physical reactions in the body, such as a faster heart beat, a rise in blood pressure, perspiration through the sweat glands, and perhaps a churning feeling in the stomach. This is a normal function of the amygdalae. Any boy who has faced down the taunts of a bully or asked the prettiest girl in class for a date would recognize those physical reactions in his body.

Scientists are now studying the amygdalae as well as other parts of the brain to see whether they can malfunction, causing the body to react to irrational fears. Similarly, scientists are studying neurotransmitters to see whether they contribute to the development of phobias. Neurotransmitters are the chemicals that flow from brain cell to brain cell, enabling messages to circulate in the brain and reach other organs of the body. Some scientists believe that imbalances in neurotransmitters may cause the brain to send out the wrong messages, such as creating a fear where one should not exist.

> " **The word *phobia* stems from the name Phobos, the ancient Greek god of fright.** "

Some Well-Known Cases

Regardless of how they are caused, the fact that some 34 million Americans suffer from either specific or social phobias indicates that phobias are quite common. Many people, including some very famous people, have few qualms about sharing their phobias with others.

Football broadcaster John Madden is one of the most familiar faces on TV. Each week during the football season, he can be seen in the broadcast booth analyzing an NFL game for a national TV audience. He is also very candid about his aviophobia, which is a fear of flying. During the football season Madden travels from city to city in a tour bus rather than endure the experience of flight.

Billionaire Howard Hughes feared germs, which means he suffered from misophobia. Hughes, who died in 1976, became so obsessed with his fear that he spent much of the last 10 years of his life locked on the top floor of a luxury hotel-casino that he owned in Las Vegas, Nevada. He came into contact with few people and took ridiculous precautions against becoming infected with germs, such as using tissues to pick up objects.

Stories about international soccer star David Beckham's fear of disorder, or ataxophobia, have often found their way into the media. Beckham has organized his closets so that each shirt hangs according to its color. He has been known to line up the soda cans that sit in his refrigerator. He often picks out clothes that match the furniture in his home. His wife, pop singer Victoria Beckham, told *People* magazine, "Everything has to match in the house. If there are three cans of Diet Coke he'd throw one away rather than having three because it's uneven."[3]

> " In most cases, people who harbor specific phobias are well aware of what frightens them, and they make special efforts to avoid their fears. "

Uncontrollable and Unpredictable

Beckham is able to deal with his phobias by making sure his closets are in order or the soda cans line up properly in the refrigerator. Some people have far less control over their lives, which means they can fall victim to their phobias at any time and experience uncontrollable panic attacks.

Beth Cox, an Atlanta, Georgia, woman, thought she had her acrophobia, or fear of heights, under control. When she took her family to the amusement park, she stayed off the roller coaster. One time, though, as her family visited Pikes Peak, she stayed in the car, huddling in terror in the back seat, while her husband and two daughters stood at the edge of the road, enjoying the awe-inspiring view of the Colorado countryside. On another occasion, Cox and a daughter embarked on a

Arachnophobia is the fear of spiders. Many people would not be able to stand having this tarantula near them.

cross-country drive over unfamiliar roads. Soon, she found herself crossing the Hernando de Soto Bridge in Memphis, Tennessee, which rises more than 100 feet above the Mississippi River. "I started hyperventilating," she told *U.S. News & World Report*. "I started going hysterical. I thought we were going to die."[4]

Cox experienced a panic attack. Her body reacted to her phobia, causing a number of debilitating symptoms, including hyperventilation, paralysis, trembling, and uncontrollable sobbing. Such reactions are common in people who suffer from phobias.

As Cox's case shows, panic attacks can be unpredictable—even people who recognize their phobias can fall victim to them. As a result, people who suffer from phobias are often chained to their disabilities; they cannot function normally and must alter their lives to accommodate their fears.

Economic Costs

Phobias take their toll on the afflicted in other ways as well. Many phobia sufferers are less productive than other people in school and at work. Studies have shown that people who suffer from social phobias are likely to earn lower wages than others. They are also less likely to go to college and enter careers in technical, professional, or managerial fields. They also call in sick a lot more than other people and tend to have higher medical bills.

> **Sufferers of social phobias also have a high incidence of substance abuse because they turn to drugs and alcohol to help them face their fears.**

Sufferers of social phobias also have a high incidence of substance abuse because they turn to drugs and alcohol to help them face their fears. Of course, drugs and alcohol do not provide the answers—they simply lead to more problems, including addiction. Moreover, people who suffer from social phobias tend to develop other, more severe mental illnesses, such as depression. Phobia sufferers also have a high rate of suicide. Said the authors of a 2001 study published in the *American Journal of Psychiatry,*

Generalized social [phobia] is associated with lower health-related quality of life, a higher rate of lifetime suicide attempts, diminished educational and occupational attainment, and higher utilization of health care resources. The magnitude of these effects and the social burden of generalized social [phobia] are similar to those of depression.[5]

Treatment Options

Despite all the obstacles that face phobia sufferers, people can learn to overcome their fears. Sometimes, all people need to do is learn how to relax. It may help if they can join a support group and talk over their phobias with others who suffer from similar fears. By comparing notes, phobia sufferers often come to the conclusion that their fears are irrational. For others, psychiatric treatment may be required. Fortunately, psychiatric therapy has proven to be successful in helping people overcome their fears.

Indeed, for sufferers of specific phobias, many people turn to cognitive-behavioral therapy, a form of treatment that has been practiced for more than 50 years. In fact, psychiatric experts believe that some people are able to overcome their specific phobias with just a handful of treatments.

In simple terms, cognitive-behavioral therapy requires the patient to take incremental steps toward overcoming his or her fears. In the first session, somebody with a fear of heights may be asked to climb a few rungs up a ladder. In the next session, the patient may be asked to climb halfway up the ladder. The therapy would continue in incremental steps until the patient is able to climb all the way to the top of the ladder without panicking. David H. Barlow, director of Boston University's Center for Anxiety and Related Disorders, told *Newsweek*, "We can take people with very severe phobias and treat them in a day or two."[6]

Others afflicted with phobias may find it necessary to take antidepressants. The drugs work by altering the flow of neurotransmitters that control emotions. Essentially, the drugs help enhance feelings of satisfaction in the patients. These drugs are particularly effective in the treatment of patients who suffer from social phobias—if they are more satisfied with themselves, they tend to have less to fear and are able to function at higher levels in social situations. However, physicians are quick to add that drug therapy is only one part of the solution and that people who suffer from social phobias also have to work closely with mental health professionals to find ways to conquer their fears on their own.

For many people it could take months or even years of professional treatment to overcome their fears. For Cox, the woman whose acrophobia could send her into a panic attack, it took months of cognitive-behavioral therapy before she was able to overcome her fear of heights. Now she enjoys taking vacations with her family and has no qualms about staying on the upper floor of a hotel. "It's not like I spend my Saturdays looking for something high," Cox told *U.S. News & World Report*, "but now when I am there, I know that I can handle it."[7]

> " **Sometimes, all people need to do is learn how to relax.** "

17

What Does the Future Hold for Phobia Sufferers?

The study of anxiety disorders, and particularly phobias, has emerged as an important field of research for physicians and mental health professionals. As such, recent discoveries about the brain and behavior have been uncovered, which have helped in the development of new drugs and recent treatment techniques.

For example, new computer technology has helped refine the science of cognitive-behavioral therapy. Now, using equipment that can simulate fearful situations through the technique known as virtual reality, patients can receive in their doctors' offices prescribed doses of what frightens them. When participating in the therapy, they wear goggles and earphones that can provide the virtual reality of crossing a very high bridge or flying in an airplane, even though they are sitting at desks in their doctors' offices. Meanwhile, the therapists can use computers to control the experiences, giving their patients just a taste of their fears. Dean McKay, director of clinical psychology at Fordham University in New York, told the journal *Inside Fordham*, "Using virtual reality therapy, you can control the feared events, exposing someone to their fears in incremental steps or picking the worst case scenario. In the absence of virtual reality therapy, you have to get on a plane and fly. There is no way to prep for it and it is impossible to plan."[8]

> By recognizing what they fear the most and finding ways to safely confront their fears, it is possible for people to overcome their phobias and lead normal and active lives.

No one questions that people with phobias experience many fears; however, a lot of evidence suggests that science is beginning to find ways to conquer people's irrational fears. By recognizing what they fear the most and finding ways to safely confront their fears, it is possible for people to overcome their phobias and lead normal and active lives.

What Are Phobias?

"About a year ago, a button came off a colleague's shirt. I ran out of the office screaming and started to hyperventilate. I can cope with small buttons, like on shirts, although I have to iron them facing the ironing board. But large plastic ones are horrible. I barely have any skirts or dresses because so many have them. Most of my trousers have drawstring waists or zippers."

—Julia Ruddick, a woman who suffers from koumpounophobia, or fear of buttons.

The world is a stressful place. The pressures of work, school, and home life can often seem too much to bear. The news can be depressing. Stories about terrorist attacks, criminal acts, economic ills, devastating hurricanes, and horrific accidents can all contribute to people's stress. Is it any wonder that many people feel anxious? Says Carolyn Chambers Clark, a health educator and author of the book *Living Well with Anxiety*, "The increased pace of modern society, the increased rate of technological change, the relative absence of traditionally prescribed values, a barrage of inconsistent world views presented in the media, terrorism threats—these and other factors make it more difficult to remain calm and to experience a sense of stability or consistency in [people's] lives."[9]

People who cannot handle stress often develop anxiety disorders. An anxiety disorder is an extreme and chronic reaction to an irrational fear, affecting a person's mood, thoughts, behavior, and activities. In many cases the condition will grow progressively worse unless it is treated.

Anxiety disorders fall into six types. Social phobias and specific phobias are two of the most common, but many people suffer from other types of anxiety disorders, including panic disorder, obsessive-compulsive disorder, post-traumatic stress disorder, and generalized anxiety disorder.

Panic disorder is a sudden attack of terror accompanied by physical symptoms, including pounding heart, perspiration, weakness, faintness, or dizziness. Other symptoms include chills, numbness, and chest pain. People who suffer from panic disorders may feel a sense of unreality and impending doom. They also feel as though they are losing control.

> " Panic disorder is a sudden attack of terror accompanied by physical symptoms, including pounding heart, perspiration, weakness, faintness, or dizziness. "

People who suffer from obsessive-compulsive disorder become obsessed with certain fears, and then develop strange rituals to deal with them. Somebody who fears intruders will lock and relock the front door perhaps dozens of times before going to bed.

Post-traumatic stress disorder afflicts many people who have suffered through a traumatic event at some point in their lives. The memory of that event can pop into their minds at any time, causing them to become irritable, aggressive, or even violent. Many veterans returning from war have suffered through episodes of post-traumatic stress disorder, but others, such as victims of crime or abuse, have experienced episodes as well.

People who suffer from generalized anxiety disorder, or GAD, are constantly worried or tense but seem to have no reason for their fretfulness. They anticipate disaster—losing their money, jobs, health, or loved ones. The constant state of worry often produces physical symptoms: GAD patients may be afflicted with constant headaches, nausea, fatigue, muscle aches, episodes of trembling, perspiration, difficulty breathing, and a constant urge to go to the bathroom.

What Is Fear?

Just because somebody is afraid of something does not mean he or she suffers from an anxiety disorder. Fear is a normal human emotion. In fact, it is a survival instinct, programmed into people's brains, enabling them to sense and respond to danger.

Fear is a common reaction to being alone or being in an unfamiliar environment. It is also a common reaction to being unsure of oneself or being vulnerable. Most people experience their first pangs of fear as young children. For example, many children are afraid of the dark. At night, even if they are in their own beds just a few feet from their parents' bedroom, they find themselves alone with their thoughts, which may be conjuring up all manner of scary, imaginary creatures. Or a sudden thunderstorm may erupt outside, creating booming and unfamiliar sounds as well as scary flashes of lightning. Or they may have gone to a friend's house for their first sleepover, where, even though they are among friends, they find themselves in unfamiliar places, surrounded by unfamiliar things.

As young people grow older, they learn to conquer their fears. They gain the confidence that comes with maturity and experience and are able to put fear into perspective. A young child who learns to conquer his or her fear of the dark soon learns to become independent, able to tread into unfamiliar environments with confidence.

> " [Generalized anxiety disorder] patients may be afflicted with constant headaches, nausea, fatigue, muscle aches, episodes of trembling, perspiration, difficulty breathing, and a constant urge to go to the bathroom. "

Fight or Flight?

Just as fear is a normal human emotion, the fight-or-flight response is a normal reaction to fear. When the brain senses danger, it sends signals to other parts of the body, preparing the other organs for a physical reaction. When the heart beats faster, it supplies the arms and legs with blood, making them stronger in case they are needed to run away or repel a physical attack. Sweat glands kick into action, providing the perspiration that helps keep the body cool. The lungs start working harder, providing the body with more oxygen it will need for a physical ordeal. Adrenaline, sugar, and other chemicals are manufactured by the body, helping produce energy, strength, stamina, and speed.

In other words, the brain has prepared the body to confront fear by staying and making a fight of it or by running away. Since the days of the cave dwellers, humans have possessed the fight-or-flight response. If the cave dweller encountered a tiger, he knew to run. If the cave dweller was armed with a spear, he may have been less fearful and stood his ground to make a fight of it. In either case, the brain prepared his body for the physical stress of fear.

> "A young child who learns to conquer his or her fear of the dark soon learns to become independent, able to tread into unfamiliar environments with confidence."

In people who suffer from phobias and other anxiety disorders, the fight-or-flight response kicks in even though the fear may be irrational. Says Reneau Z. Peurifoy, author of the book *Anxiety, Phobias, and Panic*, "When you are embarrassed and feel threatened by what others think, your body triggers the fight or flight response and begins gearing up to physically run away or fight."[10]

Two Types of Social Phobias

Social phobia is the fear of public embarrassment or humiliation. Mental health experts believe two forms of social phobia exist—circumscribed social phobia and generalized social phobia.

A circumscribed social phobia is the fear of a specific situation. Stage fright is one form of circumscribed social phobia, but the condition applies to other situations as well. For instance, many men find it impossible to urinate in a public restroom and some people are uncomfortable eating in a restaurant. Those who suffer from circumscribed social phobia are able to go to a party, but they are absolutely incapable of making small talk in a group. In the classroom, the student who suffers from circumscribed social phobia may be the person who seems least willing to raise his or her hand.

People with circumscribed social phobia often find ways to manage their phobias—they never eat in restaurants, avoid using public restrooms or, somehow, find a way to make it all the way through a term without being called on in class. Essentially, they find ways to avoid situations they fear.

People who suffer from generalized social phobia have a far more difficult time enduring life. Generalized social phobia involves fear of all social situations, such as parties, school dances, or similar events. People who suffer from the condition are very sensitive about what others say about them; they fear social gatherings because they fear they are being watched, talked about, and criticized. They try to stay out of conversations because they fear what they say will be ridiculed. Later, they may be troubled for days or even weeks by what they have said, feeling they acted like fools.

Four Types of Specific Phobias

Specific phobias, which number in the hundreds, generally fall into four categories: fear of insects and animals, fear of natural environments, fear of blood or injury, and fear of dangerous situations. "Phobias are not random," University of California at Los Angeles psychologist Michelle Craske told *Time*. "We tend to fear anything that threatens our survival as a species."[11]

Fear of insects and animals includes such common phobias as arachnophobia, the fear of spiders; ophidiophobia, the fear of snakes; and ailurophobia, the fear of cats. The fear of sharks, or selachophobia, is also a common fear. Actress Hayden Panettiere, the star of the hit TV show *Heroes*, admits to being a selachophobe. "The ocean scares the living daylights out of me," she told *Teen People*. "I love swimming, but sharks are my biggest fear. I'll suck it up and go into the water, but it's scary."[12]

Fear of blood is also known as "blood-injection-injury" phobia and could include fear of going to the doctor or dentist or receiving an inoculation. Fear of natural environments usually includes fear of heights, or acrophobia, or fear of enclosed places, which is claustrophobia. Fear of dangerous situations could include all manner of dangers, real or imagined, such as aviophobia, which is a fear of flying, or agyrophobia, fear of crossing the street.

> " **Since the days of the cave dwellers, humans have possessed the fight-or-flight response.** "

Fear of the Marketplace

Some mental health experts believe that agoraphobia, or fear of the marketplace, constitutes a third category of phobia. (The term stems from the Greek word *agora*, which means "marketplace.") Agoraphobia is the fear of open spaces, more specifically the fear of being away from a safe place. Certainly, the condition includes elements of both social and specific phobias.

One noted sufferer of agoraphobia is TV chef Paula Deen, who endured the condition for more than 20 years. In Deen's case, she believes her agoraphobia was sparked by a series of personal tragedies—both her parents died relatively young; her father, Earl, died of a stroke at the age of 40 while her mother, Corrie, died of cancer 4 years later at the age of 44. Fearing that she would die if she stepped out of the house, Deen confined herself to her home.

> "Specific phobias, which number in the hundreds, generally fall into four categories: fear of insects and animals, fear of natural environments, fear of blood or injury, and fear of dangerous situations."

In fact, during one two-month stretch in 1987 she did not even get out of bed. "Unless you've experienced it, it's hard to understand how somebody could be that fearful of fear,"[13] she told *People* magazine.

Dean eventually overcame her agoraphobia. In fact, she put the years cooped up at home to good use. She learned how to cook and published her own cookbook, which led to a career as a chef on the Food Network—after she resolved to finally leave her own house.

Many young children who suffer from a condition known as separation anxiety disorder—a fear of being separated from their homes or loved ones (usually close family members)—are likely to develop agoraphobia as adults. Although separation anxiety has long been regarded as an affliction that affects mostly young children, recent studies have shown that teenagers leaving home for college for the first time often exhibit symptoms of separation anxiety, making them prime candidates to develop agoraphobia. Indeed, some studies suggest as many as half the sufferers of separation anxiety go on to develop agoraphobia.

What Is a Panic Attack?

Before learning to overcome her agoraphobia, Deen would find herself suffering from panic attacks whenever she tried to venture out of her home. "My heart would beat so hard and my arms would be numb,"[14] she said.

For people who suffer from phobias, panic attacks can be common occurrences in their lives. Overcome by their fears, they have lost control of their emotions and, in many cases, their own bodies. The physical symptoms of a panic attack are racing pulse, pounding heart, chest pain, trembling or shaking, inability to catch one's breath, sweating, nausea, dizziness, numbness, and hot and cold flashes, among others. In addition, psychological stresses can include feelings of detachment from reality, fear of losing control, and fear of death.

Essentially, a panic attack is an uncontrollable version of the fight-or-flight response. A panic attack can arrive without warning and grow increasingly intense for 10 minutes or more. "Panic sufferers often cry out in desperation that they can't breathe; that their heart is beating in an irregular rhythm or is about to stop altogether; that their throat is closing over, that their hands and feet are becoming numb and paralyzed," says neurology professor Richard Restak. "Added to these physical sensations are fear of imminent death, feeling of unreality, and most disturbing of all, the conviction that one is losing mental control—in essence, 'going crazy.'"[15]

> " Agoraphobia is the fear of open spaces, more specifically the fear of being away from a safe place. "

"Confused, Resentful, and Agitated"

Indeed, panic attacks are no stranger to Allen Shawn. The son of noted *New Yorker* magazine editor William Shawn and brother of actor Wallace Shawn, Allen Shawn is an accomplished musician and composer. And yet, despite picking a profession that often requires him to perform in public, Shawn has for years suffered from agoraphobia as well as numerous specific phobias. In his book *Wish I Could Be There: Notes from a Phobic Life*, Shawn describes a typical panic attack that overcame him as he traveled in unfamiliar territory in search of a friend's home:

> I am driving down a dirt road in the woods to a friend's house. He didn't say how many miles down his house was. He did say it was beautiful there, on the lake. . . .

The odometer says we have been driving for four and a half miles, but the numbers have no meaning. I am growing confused and resentful and agitated. The road back will be bumpy and slow, too, I think, and wasn't there a fork back there at some point that I have already taken? How will I remember the way back? My legs are stiff and heavy, and I am trembling. I want to turn the car around. The road seems to grow darker. My muscles are coiled around one another, pulled taut. I am breaking, more and more confused, and I can't breathe. There's no sky overhead.

I turn the car around. [16]

As Shawn's experience shows, a phobia can prompt a panic attack, ruining a perfectly wonderful day in the country. Sadly, for Shawn and others who suffer from phobias, their anxiety disorders can dominate their lives, costing them good times. Meanwhile, their friends have difficulty understanding why they do not show up at parties, why they do not come out of their homes too often, or why they try so hard to avoid the eyes of the teacher as they hope someone else will be sent to the blackboard.

Primary Source Quotes*

What Are Phobias?

66 I would attend the ceremony if I were able to. But unfortunately I'm mentally ill with agoraphobia. I'm unable to be in crowds, and I can't bear to be looked at. 99

—Elfriede Jelinek, quoted in Deborah Solomon, "A Gloom of Her Own," *New York Times Magazine*, November 21, 2004, p. 31.

Jelinek won the 2004 Nobel Prize for Literature, but because of her agoraphobia, she refused to attend the ceremony in Stockholm, Sweden, to accept the award.

66 I get creeped out and I can't breathe and I can't eat around it. I've had friends tell me that maybe I was beaten to death with an antique chair in a former life. 99

—Billy Bob Thornton, quoted in Hollie McKay, "Fame-o-Phobia: What Scares the Stars?" *Fox News*, March 15, 2007. www.foxnews.com.

Thornton is an actor who harbors a fear of antiques.

* Editor's Note: While the definition of a primary source can be narrowly or broadly defined, for the purposes of Compact Research, a primary source consists of: 1) results of original research presented by an organization or researcher; 2) eyewitness accounts of events, personal experience, or work experience; 3) first-person editorials offering pundits' opinions; 4) government officials presenting political plans and/or policies; 5) representatives of organizations presenting testimony or policy.

"Being at the edge of a cliff. I always think I'm going to throw myself off—that feeling of, 'What if my body goes crazy?'"

—Dave Matthews, quoted in Danielle Anderson, "High Anxiety," *People*, February 23, 2004, p. 118..

Musician Matthews' fear of falling is known as basophobia.

"Something about the painted face, the fake smile. There always seemed to be a darkness lurking just under the surface, a potential for real evil."

—Johnny Depp, quoted in Buck Wolf, "Wolf Files: Celebrity Phobias," *ABC News,* December 16, 2003. http://abcnews.go.com.

Actor Depp admits to suffering from clourophobia, which is a fear of clowns.

"I'm scared of heights. I don't get [too] high up—I get freaked out! I mean, I do it, but I don't like it."

—James Marsden, quoted in "What's Your Phobia?" *Teen People*, September 2006, p. 37.

Marsden is an actor who suffers from acrophobia, a fear of heights.

66 Some fears are expected and explainable, like the fear of night. At night, you don't see as well, and there are predators out there. It's part of a natural response. But a phobia is a serious affliction that's stressful, debilitating, immobilizing. 99

—Carlyle Chan, quoted in Lisa Jones Townsel, "When Fear Becomes Phobias, a Wicked Web Is Spun,"
Milwaukee Journal Sentinel, October 30, 2007. www.jsonline.com.

Chan is a professor of psychology at the Medical College of Wisconsin.

66 Birds flapping around my ears. When I walk down the street with pigeons, I have to duck down. My boyfriend always laughs at me. 99

—Chloe Sevigny, quoted in Danielle Anderson, "High Anxiety," *People,* February 23, 2004, p.118.

Actress Sevigny harbors a fear of birds, or ornithophobia.

66 My phobia is deer. One time at camp, I was chased by a four-point buck. So now I sit in the house if they're outside and put my head down if I see one while [I'm] in the car. 99

—Caileigh O'Connell, quoted in "What's Your Phobia," *Teen People,* September 2006, p. 37.

O'Connell, 18, lives in Mastic Beach, New York.

66 There was no acting required. . . . It was horrific. Nobody wants to live that experience. 99

—Uma Thurman, quoted in Hollie McKay, "Fame-o-Phobia: What Scares the Stars?" *Fox News,* March 15, 2007. www.foxnews.com.

Thurman, an actress who suffers from a fear of confined spaces, or claustrophobia, once had to portray a character buried alive in the film *Kill Bill: Vol. 2.*

66 Bees are the most frightening thing in the world! Every day in middle school, I ate lunch outside, and the bees loved to follow me around. I'd freak out, scream and run every time! 99

—Kristina Pham, quoted in "What's Your Phobia?" *Teen People,* September 2006, p. 37.

Pham, 16, whose fear of bees is known as apiphobia, lives in San Jose, California.

66 I can't tell you how many carts of groceries I left sitting in the aisle at the grocery store. I had to get out of there immediately at the first sign of a panic attack. And if I didn't, I would pass out. I always had to park my car where I didn't have to back up so I could drive away fast if I felt threatened. 99

—Carolyn Archer, quoted in Chris Jones, "Left Untreated, Anxiety Disorder Can Disrupt One's Life," *Oklahoman,* October 30, 2007. http://newsok.com.

Archer, who lives in Oklahoma City, Oklahoma, was diagnosed with agoraphobia after suffering from panic attacks for two years.

66 I'm not sure what triggered it, but my dad used to go fishing and gut and clean his catch in the sink, and I would watch him do it. Soon, I was trembling and throwing up at the sight of fish. My dad had to stop eating and catching it. **99**

—Gareth Brennan, quoted in Lucy Elkins, "How I Overcame My Fish Phobia," *Daily Mail,* April 17, 2007. www.dailymail.co.uk.

Brennan, a professional singer who lives in Great Britain, suffered from ichthyophobia, or a fear of fish.

Facts and Illustrations

What Are Phobias?

- A 2007 survey of childhood fears by the University of Sheffield in England found that all **250 children** who participated in the study were **afraid of clowns**.

- *American Family Physician* magazine reports that most cases of **social phobia** develop between the **ages of 11 and 19** and that people over the age of 25 rarely exhibit their first symptoms of social phobia.

- Researchers at Carnegie Mellon University in Pittsburgh found in a 2007 study that young babies **do not fear spiders and snakes** until adults tell them they are scary.

- Despite lackluster critical reviews, the 2006 film *Snakes on a Plane*, which dramatized fear of flying and fear of snakes, garnered more than **$62 million** in worldwide box office receipts.

- As many as **20 percent** of people harbor severe phobias about **bad weather**, according to a 2006 study by the University of Iowa. The study found that people who harbor an irrational fear of the weather exhibit symptoms of dizziness, shortness of breath, nausea, and feelings of panic in the days leading up to severe storms.

- A 2003 study by Cambridge University in England found that **20 percent** of people suffer from **chrometophobia—a fear of money**. In most cases, chrometophobes fear opening envelopes that appear to be bills.

- The International Civil Aviation Organization reported the results of a study in 2007 indicating that some **40 percent** of people harbor some degree of **aviophobia**, which is a **fear of flying**.

- Psychiatrists at Mercy Hospital in Pittsburgh said in 2007 that one of the most common phobias that afflict their patients is **gephyrophobia**, which is a fear of bridges. They believe the phobia is common in Pittsburgh because it is a city in which three rivers converge.

Phobias Most Common Type of Anxiety Disorder

More than 40 million people suffer from anxiety disorders, including many people who suffer from multiple anxiety disorders. Phobias are clearly the most prevalent form of anxiety disorders, with nearly 20 million people who harbor one or more specific phobias and some 15 million people who suffer from social phobias. People who harbor specific phobias fear being embarrassed or humiliated in public places; people who harbor specific phobias possess an irrational fear that generally falls into one of 4 categories: fear of insects and animals, fear of natural environments, fear of blood or injury, and fear of dangerous situations.

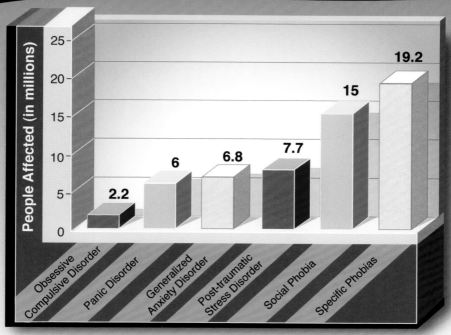

Anxiety Among College Students May Lead to Agoraphobia

Once thought to be an affliction among young children, separation anxiety disorder has been found among teenagers who leave home for the first time to attend college. A 2007 study of 190 college freshmen exhibiting symptoms of separation anxiety disorder found that many of them experience panic attacks, nightmares, insomnia, and long periods of stress and worry. As many as 50 percent of the sufferers of separation anxiety disorder may develop agoraphobia, the fear of being in crowds, public places, or open areas.

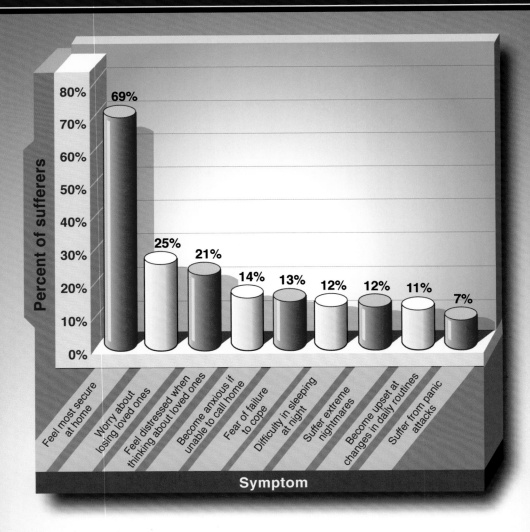

Source: Laura D. Seligman and Lisa A. Wuyek, "Correlates of Separation Anxiety Symptoms Among First-Semester College Students: An Exploratory Study," *Journal of Psychology*, March 2007.

Americans Fear Snakes the Most

More than 50 percent of the respondents to a 2001 poll by the Gallup Organization said they harbor some degree of ophidiophobia, which is the fear of snakes. Other top phobias cited in the poll included glossophobia, which is the fear of making speeches; acrophobia, a fear of heights; and claustrophobia, a fear of enclosed places.

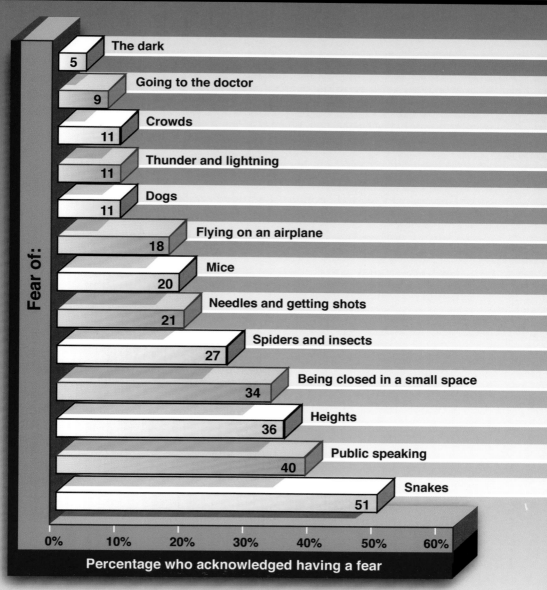

Fear of:

Fear	Percentage
The dark	5
Going to the doctor	9
Crowds	11
Thunder and lightning	11
Dogs	11
Flying on an airplane	18
Mice	20
Needles and getting shots	21
Spiders and insects	27
Being closed in a small space	34
Heights	36
Public speaking	40
Snakes	51

Percentage who acknowledged having a fear

Source: Geoffrey Brewer, "Snakes Top List of Americans' Fears," Gallup Organization, March 19, 2001. www.gallup.com.

- African Americans suffer from **higher rates of agoraphobia** than members of other ethnic groups, according to a 2007 study by Saint Louis University in Missouri. Authors of the study theorized that African Americans often live in crime-ridden neighborhoods and, therefore, have much to fear when they venture outdoors.

- According to the Stress Management Center and Phobia Institute of Asheville, North Carolina, as many as **21 million** Americans harbor some degree of **paraskevidekatriaphobia**, which is the **fear of Friday the thirteenth**, the *Wilkes-Barre Citizens' Voice* reported in 2007.

- Due to the terrorist attacks of 2001 and other terrorist-related incidents, many people who live in Europe have developed **Islamophobia**, which is a **fear of Muslims**, according to the Vienna, Austria–based European Monitoring Center on Racism and Xenophobia. The 2006 report likened Islamophobia to **xenophobia, which is a fear of strangers or foreigners**.

- At least **four presidents of the United States** are known to have harbored **anxiety disorders**, according to a 2006 study by psychiatrists at Duke University in North Carolina. The study found that Lyndon B. Johnson and Woodrow Wilson suffered from generalized anxiety disorder, while Calvin Coolidge and Thomas Jefferson endured social phobia.

- **Little Miss Muffet** may have been literature's **first arachnophobe**. The nursery rhyme featuring the little girl who was frightened by a spider was first published in 1805.

- Most people who suffer from **emetophobia—a fear of vomiting**—are women, according to a 2006 study reported in the journal *Behavioral and Cognitive Psychotherapy*. In addition, the study found that emetophobia is very difficult to overcome: Most emetophobes continue to fear vomiting for 25 years or more.

- The **fear of intruders** or burglars—known as **scelerophobia**—has prompted many upscale California homeowners to construct **"panic rooms"** in their homes, the *San Francisco Chronicle* reported in 2002. The rooms are secure, locked facilities equipped with bathrooms, food lockers, and other components that can protect occupants for weeks.

What Causes Phobias?

❝Most of us have a sense of repulsion if we meet with a snake. Snake phobia, we might say, is universal.❞

—Psychoanalyst Sigmund Freud.

P hobias have been a part of human history for at least 2,500 years. The ancient Greek physician Hippocrates, who lived in the fifth century B.C., first noted the symptoms of phobias in a patient who chose to leave home at night only, when the streets were deserted, keeping to the shadows. If forced to leave home during the day, Hippocrates observed, the man would cover his face so he could not be recognized by others. In another patient, Hippocrates noticed the man never attended parties or other public events. The patient, Hippocrates wrote, "dared not come in company for fear he would be misused, disgraced, overshoot himself in gesture or speech, or be sick; he thinks every man observes him, aims at him, derides him, owes him malice."[17] Both men, Hippocrates wrote, "fear that which need not be feared."[18]

Clearly, both patients suffered from social phobia—a malady that Hippocrates would observe in many more patients. What is more, Hippocrates also identified agoraphobia and many specific phobias in a number of patients. Hippocrates wrote that one patient, Damocles, harbored a fear of heights. Damocles "could not go near a precipice, or over a bridge, or beside even the shallowest ditch," wrote the physician, "and yet he could walk in the ditch itself."[19]

Hippocrates was not sure what caused phobias. He suspected the cause was not entirely mental, that people harbored irrational fears for physiological reasons. Some 2,500 years later, modern science has proven him correct.

Women Suffer Most

Today, more than 19 million Americans are afflicted with specific phobias, while some 15 million Americans exhibit symptoms of social phobia. Social phobias affect men and women in roughly equal numbers, but studies show that women suffer from specific phobias in far larger numbers than men—some estimates suggest as many as 9 of 10 specific phobia sufferers are female. Women also suffer from agoraphobia in larger numbers than men—some estimates suggest women suffer from agoraphobia at 4 times the rate of men. Helen Saul, author of *Phobias: Fighting the Fear*, believes women are particularly vulnerable to agoraphobia because of their places in society. "Life may actually be more dangerous for women," she says, adding:

> " Social phobias affect men and women in roughly equal numbers, but studies show that women suffer from specific phobias in far larger numbers than men. "

They are more vulnerable to physical and sexual abuse than men. Women are the ones who get pregnant, and an unwanted pregnancy is a more serious issue for the woman involved than the man. They also tend to look after small children; anyone with this responsibility might be especially aware of the dangers on the streets and more loath than usual to go out.[20]

Phobias often become apparent in preadolescence and tend to stay with people as they grow into adults—a trend that may help explain why women suffer the most from phobias. Indeed, Saul believes it may be partially the fault of parents who tend to be more protective of daughters than sons. She says parents often encourage boys to exert themselves and be independent, while girls are urged to play it safe and stay close to home. "A boy who gets a cut lip in a game is heroic, and any scar will make him more attractive and masculine," she says. "If a girl has the same injury, everyone worries that the scar will mar her for life."[21]

Little Hans

Over the centuries many physicians observed phobias in their patients without really knowing what caused them or what to do about them. Finally, in 1909, Sigmund Freud, the Austrian physician who established psychiatry as a modern science, theorized that phobias and other irrational thoughts were prompted by sexual urges. Freud had encountered a five-year-old boy who harbored a pronounced fear of horses. Freud suggested that "Little Hans" had an oedipal complex (the word is drawn from the Greek tragedy of Oedipus, the son who had sex with his mother), and that Hans's hatred for his father and love for his mother manifested itself in an irrational fear of horses. Wrote Freud, "The main point of the problem of phobias seems to me that phobias do not occur at all when the [sexual development] is normal."[22]

Freud developed his theory after interviewing Hans just once and, in his analysis, completely ignored the fact that the boy had recently witnessed a horrific collision on the street in which a horse was struck by a bus. Nevertheless, to cure the boy of his fear of horses, Freud told his parents that they should encourage Hans to talk about his troubles, which they did. They learned that Hans felt isolated and alone because his mother had gotten pregnant again and had been paying less attention to him.

Thirteen years later, Freud encountered Hans again. Now a young man, Freud found Hans to be well-adjusted and no longer harboring fears about horses. In fact, after questioning his former patient, Freud learned that Hans had no memory of his childhood phobia.

> **Phobias often become apparent in pre-adolescence and tend to stay with people as they grow into adults.**

It is difficult to argue with Freud's solution—today, support groups for phobia sufferers encourage patients to talk about what troubles them—but as important as Freud has been to the science of mental illness, his theory that phobias are prompted by sexual desires has generally been discarded by most mental health experts, who have found no factual basis in the theory at all.

Albert B. and the Theory of Behaviorism

In fact, American psychologists John B. Watson and Rosalie Raynor started the movement to debunk Freud's theory just 11 years later when they published the findings of a study they had launched involving a baby named "Albert B." In the study, Albert was encouraged to play happily by himself. After a time, Watson and Raynor showed Albert a little white laboratory rat—harmless for all intents and purposes—but when the rat was introduced to Albert, Watson and Raynor clanged an iron bar behind Albert's head. The sudden loud noise frightened the boy. A few days later, they showed the rat to Albert again, this time without making the noise. Wrote Watson and Raynor, "He first began to fret and then covered his eyes with both hands."[23] Clearly, Albert was frightened of the white rat—just as Hans was frightened of horses because of his memory of the terrible accident.

> "Sigmund Freud . . . theorized that phobias and other irrational thoughts were prompted by sexual urges."

Essentially, Watson and Raynor showed that irrational fears can be prompted by a single traumatic event or series of events in the life of a person. This theory is known as behaviorism. Over the years, other anxiety disorders have been attributed to behaviorism as well; for example, participants in warfare or other violent experiences often suffer from post-traumatic stress disorder—the traumatic incidents in their memories suddenly reappear to dominate their thoughts, causing them to become anxious, agitated, or even violent.

Today, behaviorism is regarded as one of the primary psychological sources of irrational fear. Indeed, most people who harbor specific phobias can look back in time and recall a single incident or series of incidents that led to their fear of dogs, heights, water, or any number of other things. But science has also shown that while an adult's phobia of dogs may stem from an incident in which he or she was chased or bitten by a dog in childhood, that unfortunate incident in the individual's past is not the only cause.

Physiological Factors

In recent years physicians have studied the amygdalae, the almond-shaped components of the brain that control many emotions, including the reaction to fear. Each person has two—they are located a few inches from the ears. It is the amygdalae that signal the body to respond to fear, causing the heart to beat faster, lungs to work harder, sweat glands to kick in, and so on. In an interview with *U.S. News & World Report*, New York University neuroscientist Joseph LeDoux called the amygdala "the hub in the wheel of fear."[24]

When it comes to fear, though, other parts of the brain also take action. One part of the brain, the hippocampus, stores memories. And so when a person encounters a fearful situation, the hippocampus conjures up a memory of a similar incident in the past while the amygdalae respond by preparing the body for the physical stress of the ordeal. Finally, a third part of the brain takes action as well. This is the prefrontal cortex, which regulates rational and analytical thought. It is the prefrontal cortex that assesses the situation and decides the seriousness of the danger.

Therefore, if the amygdalae, hippocampus, and prefrontal cortex do not function properly or in sync, the brain could develop an overreaction to the danger, treating it irrationally. The body may overreact as well, perhaps with a panic attack.

Several recent studies have focused on the roles of the amygdalae, hippocampus, and prefrontal cortex in the development of phobias and have concluded that abnormalities in those parts of the brain may be at the root of irrational fear.

> " Watson and Raynor showed that irrational fears can be prompted by a single traumatic event or series of events in the life of a person.

Physiological factors may also explain why women suffer more from phobias than men. In 1999 a study published in the *Journal of Clinical Psychiatry* reported that female hormones may be a reason for irrational fears in women. The study said many women report feelings of anxiety right before the onset of their menstrual periods, a time when the female hormones estrogen and progesterone are thrown out of balance.

Neurotransmitter Abnormalities

Meanwhile, some mental health experts are exploring the role neurotransmitters may play in creating irrational fears. Neurotransmitters are chemicals manufactured by the brain that carry messages from one brain cell, or neuron, to the other. Their messages instruct the feet how to walk, the mouth how to form words, the fingers how to grasp a fork or spoon, the heart how to beat, and the body how to perform thousands of other functions.

Neurotransmitters also play a role in regulating emotions, prompting some experts to suggest that a neurotransmitter imbalance could help foster anxiety and irrational fears. Among the neurotransmitters that are being studied for their effect on anxiety disorders are dopamine, which helps regulate mood, attention, motor activity, and learning; norepinephrine, which controls attention and concentration; and serotonin, which helps regulate anger and aggression. Indeed, serotonin is believed to be very active in cases in which the body senses danger; it is employed by the brain to control the body's reaction to a threat. Said Restak "Serotonin plays a major role in the production of anxiety. People with low levels of serotonin are prone both to excessive anxiety and exaggerated, often inappropriate displays of aggression."[25]

> If the amygdalae, hippocampus, and prefrontal cortex do not function properly or in sync, the brain could develop an overreaction to the danger, treating it irrationally.

Clearly, researchers are studying many physiological factors that may account for the creation of irrational fears: Phobias could stem from abnormalities in the brain or in the chemicals—the hormones and neurotransmitters—that perform important functions in the regulation of emotions. But people may develop irrational fears that have nothing to do with a deep and dark childhood memory, a serotonin imbalance, or a malfunctioning cerebral cortex.

Are Phobias Inherited?

Why is arachnophobia, a fear of spiders, a common phobia, while ombrophobia, the fear of rain, much less common? The answer may lie in evolution: Years ago, people's ancestors learned to be afraid of spiders and passed on that trait in their DNA. Far fewer people were afraid of rain;

therefore, ombrophobia was passed on to far fewer descendants. A study performed in 2000 by the National Institute of Mental Health found that identical twins frequently suffer from similar anxiety disorders, while fraternal twins, whose genetic history is not quite as similar, generally do not. "Genes are the template from which we develop. They influence all aspects of our physical and mental well-being, including our appearance and vulnerability to diseases, our intelligence and personality," said Saul. "Genes certainly influence the development of the brain's structure and the activity of chemical messengers involved in our experience of fear."[26]

> " Serotonin is believed to be very active in cases in which the body senses danger; it is employed by the brain to control the body's reaction to a threat. "

Certainly, it is possible that people's phobias are prompted by a variety of sources—psychological, physical, and genetic. Albert may have been frightened when Watson and Raynor clanged the iron bar behind his head, but it is also possible that Albert's amygdalae and hippocampus were not working in sync and that his serotonin was seriously out of balance. Also, Albert's ancestors may have been afraid of rodents. And had Albert been a young girl, there may have been social factors involved in her irrational fear of that little white rat.

What Causes Phobias?

Primary Source Quotes

> "White rat suddenly taken from the basket and presented to Albert. He began to reach for rat with left hand. Just as his hand touched the animal the bar was struck immediately behind his head. The infant jumped violently and fell forward, burying his face in the mattress. He did not cry, however."

—John B. Watson and Rosalie Rayner, notes from the Albert B. experiment, excerpted from "Conditioned Emotional Reactions," *Journal of Experimental Psychology*, 1920, reprinted in *Classics in the History of Psychology*, York University, Toronto, Ontario. http://psychclassics.yorku.ca.

Psychologists Watson and Rayner developed the theory of behaviorism, suggesting that unpleasant experiences are at the root of many people's fears.

....

> "Complex memories are spread across hundreds of thousands of neurons. The same neurons can participate in many memories."

—Joseph LeDoux, quoted in Michael Behar, "Paging Dr. Fear," *Popular Science*, January 2008, p. 50.

LeDoux is a neuroscientist at New York University.

....

* Editor's Note: While the definition of a primary source can be narrowly or broadly defined, for the purposes of Compact Research, a primary source consists of: 1) results of original research presented by an organization or researcher; 2) eyewitness accounts of events, personal experience, or work experience; 3) first-person editorials offering pundits' opinions; 4) government officials presenting political plans and/or policies; 5) representatives of organizations presenting testimony or policy.

66 **Nothing so fixes a thing so intensely in the memory as the wish to forget it.** 99

—Michel de Montaigne, quoted in Allen Shawn, *Wish I Could Be There: Notes from a Phobic Life.* New York: Viking, 2007, p. 150.

De Montaigne was a sixteenth-century French philosopher and essayist.

66 **The amygdala acts as a protection device. It is designed to detect and avoid danger. If the animal encounters a predator such as a snake, the amygdala assesses the snake as a threat.** 99

—David Amaral, quoted in Richard Restak, *Poe's Heart and the Mountain Climber: Exploring the Effect of Anxiety on Our Brains and Our Culture.* New York: Harmony, 2004, pp. 93–94.

Amaral is a neuroscientist and editor of the scientific journal *Amygdala* and director of the California Regional Primate Research Center at the University of California–Davis.

66 **A memory is preserved in a plastic state. You can sculpt it or update it. Theoretically, any memory, including a fear or declarative memory—being able to say what you had for breakfast yesterday—is capable of being modified.** 99

—Roger Pitman, quoted in Michael Behar, "Paging Dr. Fear," *Popular Science*, January 2008, p. 50.

Pitman is a professor of psychology at Harvard University.

66 Two people can go through the exact same traumatic event, but the high-strung, emotionally sensitive person is more vulnerable to the fear. **99**

—Michelle Craske, quoted in Jeffrey Kluger et al., "Fear Not!," *Time,* April 2, 2001, p. 52.

Craske is a psychologist in the University of California at Los Angeles Anxiety and Behavioral Disorders Program.

66 The amygdala, in addition to being a storehouse of primitive and intense memories and a center for response to threats, is crucial for the attachment of emotional significance to things. **99**

—Allen Shawn, *Wish I Could Be There: Notes from a Phobic Life.* New York: Viking, 2007, p. 62.

Shawn, a writer, musician, and composer, suffers from social and specific phobias and is the author of *Wish I Could Be There: Notes from a Phobic Life.*

66 There is a legitimacy to the idea that phobias can be learned. We respond to what we see or experience. **99**

—Edna B. Foa, quoted in Jeffrey Kluger et al., *Time,* April 2, 2001, p. 52.

Foa is a professor of psychiatry and psychology in the University of Pennsylvania.

❝Scientists have combed the 140 pages' worth of analysis of Little Hans and found no evidence that the boy sexually desired his mother . . . but the link between sex and phobias, started by Freud, has hampered phobia treatment for decades.❞

—Helen Saul, *Phobias: Fighting the Fear.* New York: Arcade, 2001, p. 33.

Saul is a medical and science journalist based in Great Britain and author of the book *Phobias: Fighting the Fear.*

❝When your serotonin level is low, depression usually follows. When your brain produces serotonin, tension and anxiety are eased. When your brain produces dopamine or norepinephrine, you are more alert and react more quickly.❞

—Carolyn Chambers Clark, *Living Well with Anxiety.* New York: HarperCollins, 2006, p. 38.

Clark is a health educator and author of the book *Living Well with Anxiety.*

❝The amygdala tells the rest of the brain, 'Hey, whatever happened, make a strong memory of it.' It makes a strong correlation between the significance of an event and the remembrance of it.❞

—James McGaugh, quoted in Geoffrey Cowley et al., "Our Bodies, Our Fears," *Newsweek,* February 24, 2003, p. 42.

McGaugh is a neurobiologist at the University of California at Irvine.

"Show a baby a picture of a spider, and it will instinctively pull away. However, a baby would not shy away from a picture of a rabbit or a kitten. This is because we have evolved to be afraid of poisonous or dangerous animals or situations. It is in our DNA."

—Felix Economakis, quoted in Lucy Elkins, "How I Overcame My Fish Phobia," *Daily Mail,* April 17, 2007. www.dailymail.co.uk.

Economakis is a British psychologist and frequent guest on the BBC television program *The Panic Room*, which explores phobias.

What Causes Phobias?

- An experiment at New York University found that in rats, the **auditory thalamus**—the part of the brain that receives signals from the ears—is linked directly to the amygdalae, *Popular Science* reported in 2008. When the scientists **surgically cut the link**, they discovered the rats were no longer afraid of threatening sounds because they no longer had a memory of fear.

- Many scientists believe there is a **"phobia gene,"** meaning that phobias are passed down from generation to generation; according to *Time*, **40 percent** of all people who suffer from a specific phobia have at least one parent who also suffers from a phobia.

- An Australian study found that **25 percent** of agoraphobia sufferers have close relatives who are agoraphobic, author Helen Saul reports in her book, *Phobias: Fighting the Fear*.

- The science journal *Nature* published the results of a study in 2001 indicating phobias are learned: When some participants were told to simply expect an **electrical shock**, they responded with as much fear as those who actually did receive the shocks.

- The time it takes for the amygdalae to transmit signals of fear to the rest of the body has been measured in **milliseconds**, according to *Newsweek*.

- According to *Time*, **55 percent** of social phobia sufferers are women. Also, women make up as much as **90 percent** of specific phobia sufferers, the magazine reported.

- *Newsweek* reported that during the Persian Gulf War in 1991 some **100 Israelis died of heart attacks** prompted by the fear of Scud missile attacks launched by Iraq; none of those victims had actually been injured by the missile blasts.

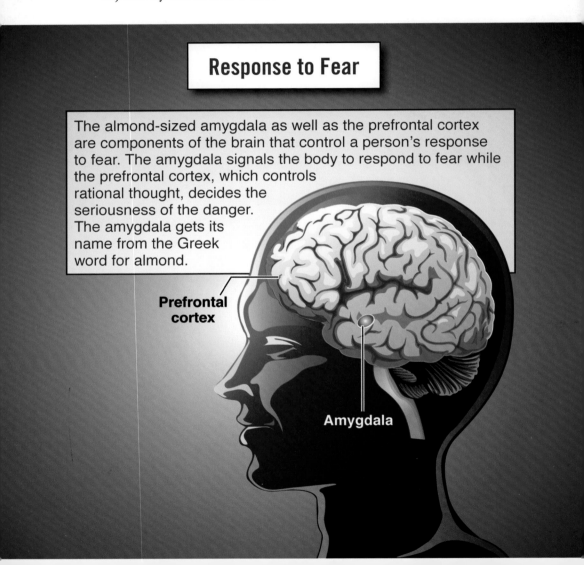

Response to Fear

The almond-sized amygdala as well as the prefrontal cortex are components of the brain that control a person's response to fear. The amygdala signals the body to respond to fear while the prefrontal cortex, which controls rational thought, decides the seriousness of the danger. The amygdala gets its name from the Greek word for almond.

Prefrontal cortex

Amygdala

Memories and Phobias

The hippocampus is the component of the brain that stores memories, including memories of what people fear. The hippocampus feeds those memories to the amygdalae, which respond by bracing the body for a fearful situation. Abnormalities in the amygdalae, hippocampus, and other parts of the brain may result in phobias. The hippocampus gets its name from the Greek word for seahorse. When viewed in a cross-section, the hippocampus is said to resemble a seahorse.

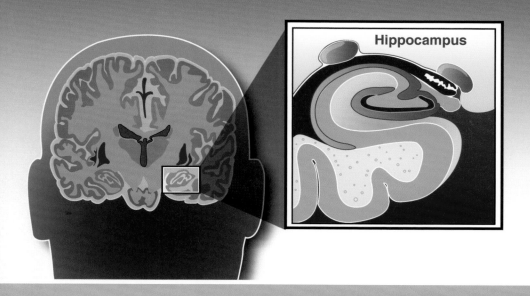

Hippocampus

Sources: University of Wisconsin Graduate School, www.graduateschool.uwm.edu; Monroe Street Medical Clinic, "Medicine for People," 2007.www.rienstraclinic.com.

- By photographing images of the brains of volunteers, Australian researchers found that the **amygdalae become hyperactive** when the volunteers observed faces they perceived as threatening, angry, disgusted, or fearful, the journal *Biological Psychiatry* reported in 2006. The researchers believe the amygdalae react similarly in social phobia patients.

How the Body Processes Fear

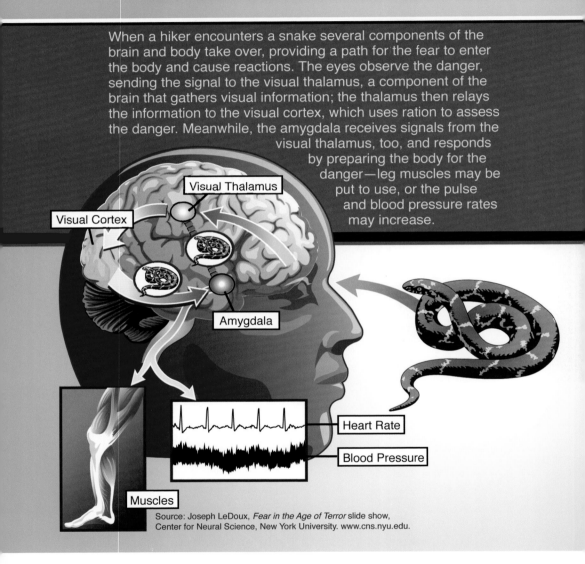

When a hiker encounters a snake several components of the brain and body take over, providing a path for the fear to enter the body and cause reactions. The eyes observe the danger, sending the signal to the visual thalamus, a component of the brain that gathers visual information; the thalamus then relays the information to the visual cortex, which uses ration to assess the danger. Meanwhile, the amygdala receives signals from the visual thalamus, too, and responds by preparing the body for the danger—leg muscles may be put to use, or the pulse and blood pressure rates may increase.

Visual Thalamus

Visual Cortex

Amygdala

Heart Rate

Blood Pressure

Muscles

Source: Joseph LeDoux, *Fear in the Age of Terror* slide show, Center for Neural Science, New York University. www.cns.nyu.edu.

• The prefrontal cortex, which controls rational thought, may have a large impact on learned fear. A 2007 study published by the *Journal of Neuroscience* reported that scientists in Puerto Rico were able to remove a lab rat's learned fear of loud noises by **chemically deadening** activity in the prefrontal cortex, but the experiment had no effect on the **rat's natural fear of a cat**.

- The journal *Nature Neuroscience* reported in 2007 that a lack of serotonin in mice causes them to **misinterpret ambiguous signals**—an indication that a phobia sufferer whose brain produces an insufficient supply of the neurotransmitter may misinterpret a normal situation as one he or she should fear.

Phobias Caused by Out of Sync Brain

The amygdala, hippocampus, and prefrontal cortex all play roles in how the body responds to fear. When the amygdala receives a stimulus, such as the image of a spider, it draws on the memories of the spider stored in the hippocampus as well as the assessment of the spider's danger provided by the prefrontal cortex. After just a few milliseconds, the amygdala decides how to respond to the threat by providing an emotional response. It is believed that phobias are caused when these brain functions do not act in sync.

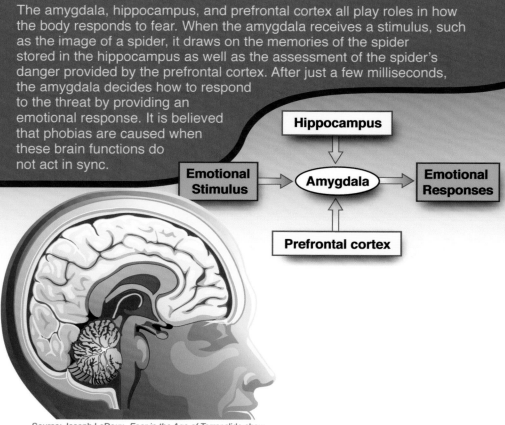

Hippocampus

Emotional Stimulus → **Amygdala** → **Emotional Responses**

Prefrontal cortex

Source: Joseph LeDoux, *Fear in the Age of Terror* slide show, Center for Neural Science, New York University. www.cns.nyu.edu.

- A phobic person may have an abundance of a certain protein in his or her **hippocampus**, the part of the brain that stores memories; a 2008 study by Rockefeller University in New York found that mice lacking the protein, which is known as tissue plasminogen activator, were braver than those with the protein.

- A person who suffers from social phobia may suffer damage to his or her hippocampus; a 2007 study by Rosalind Franklin University of Medicine in Illinois found brain cells had died in the hippocampuses of rats following **stressful social contacts** with other rats. The scientists who performed the study theorized that similar reactions in people could lead to depression and other mental illnesses.

- A 2001 study by Wayne State University Medical School in Michigan concluded that **caffeine**, the active ingredient in coffee and chocolate, **may cause a chemical imbalance** in the brain that could manifest itself in phobias, *Cosmopolitan* reported.

How Do Phobias Affect People?

> ❝ I'm not afraid of death, but I don't want to go to the hospital. You have to help me stay out of the hospital. ❞

—Artist Andy Warhol's plea to his doctor shortly before he died of complications from an infected gallbladder.

Anxiety disorders, particularly social phobia, can take their toll on people, their families, and society. Recent studies have shown that social phobia can have an effect on the workplace, the economy, and people's relationships.

Mostly, though, phobias affect only the people who suffer from them. People who are afflicted with social phobia have low self-esteem and virtually no social lives. They stay away from others because they fear them.

In an interview with *Time*, Philadelphia psychologist Richard G. Heimberg recalled treating a 50-year-old patient who had never been in a romantic relationship because he feared rejection so much he could never summon the courage to ask a woman for a date. The man longed for companionship—he wanted to get married and start a family. Heimberg worked with the patient for several months, convincing him to ask a woman for a date. Finally, the man summoned the courage and, much to his astonishment, the woman accepted.

The next day, Heimberg asked the patient whether he enjoyed himself on the date. Yes, the patient said, he had. But when Heimberg asked the patient whether he would ask the woman out again, the patient replied that he would not. "She's only going to give to charity once,"[27] he said.

Clearly, Heimberg had a lot more work to do with his patient. Even after enjoying a successful evening with the woman, the patient still felt a tremendous fear that he would be rejected if he asked his friend to go out with him a second time. And the only person who truly suffered was the man himself, who had to spend another lonely night at home. Said Heimberg in an interview with the journal *Monitor on Psychology*, "Some people think they are just shy—that it's a personality trait—and that's just the way they are. But if a person starts fearing many social situations, and as a result lives alone or drops out of school, that's not a shyness—that's an impairment."[28]

Economic Impact

Constantly living in fear and loneliness can take a physical toll on the body. In 2001 Dean Health Plan, an insurance company that provides health insurance to some 180,000 workers, released the results of a study that focused on whether people with social phobia get sick more often than other people. The study concluded that they do.

The study found that patients who suffer from social phobia spend more than $2,500 a year on their own health care, about $700 more than others. They tend to suffer from more ailments, aches, and diseases than others, possibly because their immunities are compromised by the stresses they live under. The study also found they tend to suffer longer—it takes people who harbor irrational fears longer to recover from ailments than people who do not suffer from phobias.

> **People who suffer from phobias place more stress on the health-care system, forcing insurers to pay more for their care.**

It means that people who suffer from phobias place more stress on the health-care system, forcing insurers to pay more for their care—which helps drive up the costs of medical care for others. Moreover, since they tend to call in sick more often than other employees, they miss more days of work. The Dean Health Plan study found that social phobia sufferers have sick rates 60 percent higher than others. In addition, when they do report for work the study found that they are about half as productive as their coworkers.

Such circumstances often cost their employers, who generally pay employees who are out sick. Meanwhile, at work, the employers must find ways to cover for the ill or unproductive employees—either putting an extra burden on other employees or hiring temporary workers.

Underachievers

Of course, people who suffer from social phobia are also holding themselves back. By not being good employees, they give up opportunities for advancement. Indeed, the Dean Health Plan study found that people who suffer from social phobia are less likely to finish college and less likely to obtain a job in a profession or skilled trade than others. Also, their wages will be lower than people who do not suffer from social phobia. Said the authors of the study:

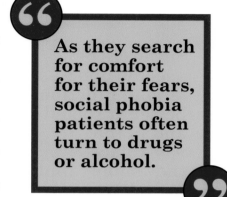

As they search for comfort for their fears, social phobia patients often turn to drugs or alcohol.

> The average subject with [social phobia] disorder has a probability of graduating from college that is 10 percentage points lower and earns wages that are 10 percent lower than persons without [social phobia] disorder. In addition, the probability that a person with average-severe [social phobia] disorder holds a technical, professional, or managerial job is 14 percentage points lower than that of an otherwise healthy individual. Combined with our observation that [social phobia] disorder can begin in pre-adolescence, these findings underscore the profound effect on lifetime achievement.[29]

Other studies have produced similar results. In 1999 the journal *American Family Physician* reported the results of a study that found as many as 85 percent of social phobia sufferers experience some degree of difficulty in school or in the workplace that impedes their abilities to perform. "In one sample," the journal reported, "nearly one half of those with social phobia were unable to complete high school; 70 percent were in the lowest [quarter] or socioeconomic status, and approximately 22 percent were on welfare."[30]

Spiraling Downward

As they search for comfort for their fears, social phobia patients often turn to drugs or alcohol. In fact, the Dean Health Plan study found that social phobia patients suffer higher degrees of alcohol abuse than patients who suffer from other forms of anxiety disorder, such as obsessive-compulsive disorder or post-traumatic stress disorder. The *American Family Physician* article reported that as many as 16 percent of social phobia patients abuse alcohol—more than three times the rate found in the general population.

> **Sufferers of specific phobias tend to function better at school and in the workplace— they simply find ways to avoid their fears.**

Social phobia and other anxiety disorders can lead to other mental illnesses, particularly depression. Depression is a mental illness characterized by feelings of sadness, hopelessness, and inadequacy but is not necessarily prompted by irrational fears. People who suffer from depression often cannot summon the energy to rise from their beds.

Suicide rates are also higher for social phobia sufferers. The Dean Health Plan study found that 22 percent of people who suffer from social phobia admitted to attempting suicide at some point in their lives, which was similar to the attempted suicide rate among depression sufferers. Summing it all up, the Dean Health Plan study said,

> [Social phobia] disorder is associated with lower-related quality of life, a higher rate of lifetime suicides, diminished educational and occupational attainment, and higher utilization of health care resources. The magnitude of these effects and the societal burden of [social phobia] disorder are similar to those of depression.[31]

Fear of the Dentist

Sufferers of specific phobias tend to function better at school and in the workplace—they simply find ways to avoid their fears and in most cases are able to adjust their lives around their phobias. But some specific phobias can lead to tragedy.

In 1999 a Welsh physician, James Kidd, lost his job at a hospital because of drug abuse. Twice, Kidd had been found unconscious in his car after taking heavy dosages of a sedative. Shortly after losing his job, Kidd committed suicide by taking a drug overdose.

The investigation into Kidd's death revealed the startling fact that the physician suffered from dentophobia—a fear of the dentist—and had not seen a dentist in 10 years. On the two occasions Kidd passed out in his car, he had driven to the dentist's office and had taken the sedatives while sitting in the parking lot. Clearly, he had been using the drugs to calm his nerves before walking into the dentist's office—in both cases, though, he passed out.

Ian Edwards, the coroner who conducted the investigation into Kidd's death, told the BBC, "James Kidd was a doctor whose skill and professionalism were beyond reproach. Yet he had a weakness, and that weakness was that he was human. He had a deep-rooted fear of dentists."[32]

Finally, Kidd took his own life. Humiliated and depressed by the loss of his job, Kidd checked into a motel, locked the door, and took a fatal dose of drugs. "He lost his job but it was not just a job," Edwards told the BBC. "This was his professional integrity. It was his purpose in life. It proved an impossible burden to bear."[33]

BII Phobias

Kidd's story illustrates the unique problems faced by sufferers of BII, or "blood-injection-injury" phobias. Indeed, Kidd harbored a BII phobia even though he had worked for years as a physician.

People with specific phobias tend to avoid their fears, but if they harbor a BII phobia they can also do harm to themselves. People with BII phobias are afraid of blood and needles. In Kidd's case, he endured years of dental problems but could not bring himself to sit in a dentist's chair. Others who harbor BII phobias may ignore the symptoms of much more serious health issues and even put their lives in danger.

> " People with specific phobias tend to avoid their fears, but if they harbor a BII phobia they can also do harm to themselves. "

That is what happened to artist Andy Warhol. He was an icon of the pop art movement of the 1960s and 1970s—his painted images of soup cans and soap pad boxes made art history. In late 1986 Warhol noticed a pain in his side. He continued to ignore the symptoms, even though they were growing progressively worse. He ached constantly, lost his appetite, and found himself unable to summon much energy. In the meantime, he somehow managed to maintain a busy schedule.

His friends certainly noticed his illness, but they also noticed something else about Warhol: He harbored a deep degree of nosocomephobia, a fear of hospitals. One of his friends, Benjamin Liu, told Warhol's biographer Bob Colacello that Warhol's fear of hospitals became evident whenever he took a taxicab ride with the artist. "Whenever we would pass a hospital, he would cover his eyes or block his view,"[34] Liu said.

> **Had Warhol sought the advice of a doctor soon after he started feeling pain in his side, he may have suffered far fewer complications from what should have been a routine medical procedure.**

In February 1987 Warhol finally consented to see a doctor who quickly diagnosed the illness as gallstones—a common condition in which bile hardens and accumulates in the gallbladder, an organ that stores bile, which the body uses to facilitate digestion. In many cases, doctors recommend the surgical removal of the gallbladder. It is a routine surgery with a high degree of success. Since Warhol let his condition persist for so long, the doctor found that his gallbladder had been infected and recommended that Warhol immediately undergo the surgery. The doctor was concerned that his gallbladder could burst, which could lead to a more widespread infection in the body and possibly even death. But the artist still delayed, unable to find the courage to walk through the front doors of a hospital. Finally, a day later, Warhol asked some friends to take him to the hospital. The next morning, doctors removed his gallbladder—by now, it was gangrenous, meaning it was severely infected. Following the operation, Warhol's condition seemed to improve at first, but that evening he took a bad turn and died from a heart attack.

Had Warhol sought the advice of a doctor soon after he started feeling pain in his side, he may have suffered far fewer complications from what should have been a routine medical procedure. But his irrational fear of hospitals caused his condition to grow worse, which undoubtedly played a role in his death.

Traumatic Events

Sometimes phobias can be sparked by a single cataclysmic event and seem to sweep through a community. The terrorist attacks of 2001 led to many cases of fear of flying. More recently, the collapse of the Interstate 35W bridge in Minneapolis led to many cases of gephyrophobia, which is the fear of bridges.

The Minneapolis bridge collapsed suddenly on August 1, 2007, plunging dozens of cars into the Mississippi River below. Thirteen people died in the tragedy. For days, horrific scenes of the collapse and the rescue efforts were broadcast on national television and featured in other media as well. Meanwhile, state and city governments ordered inspections of bridges elsewhere—news events that were covered by the media. Those images made an indelible mark in the minds of many people, who suddenly found themselves filled with dread as they approached bridges. Brooklyn, New York, psychologist Alan Hilfer told ABC News, "The anxiety of people certainly could be kicked up by [the bridge collapse], and a small percentage of people who had anxiety before may move into the phobic category."[35]

> " People who suffer from phobias find that their fears often have a pronounced effect on their own lives—they are more prone to miss work, drop out of school, earn less money, and get sick more often. "

Indeed, within days of the event journalists reported many cases of gephyrophobia. "My temperature changes and then all of a sudden I think I'm getting over the bridge and I realize I'm not thinking clearly,"[36] U.S. State

Department employee Elise Ayers told CBS News about crossing the four-mile-long Chesapeake Bay Bridge in Maryland.

Clearly, phobias have a way of dominating many people's lives—and not just the people who find themselves harboring fears as they cross bridges soon after an accident. People who suffer from phobias find that their fears often have a pronounced effect on their own lives—they are more prone to miss work, drop out of school, earn less money, and get sick more often. And some phobia sufferers, such as James Kidd and Andy Warhol, may have paid the ultimate price for harboring fears that were irrational yet by no means harmless.

How Do Phobias Affect People?

66 It's not so much a fear of the bridge. It's a fear of being on the bridge, being halfway across the bridge and suddenly panicking and thinking, 'I want to get off. What if I pass out? What if I die?' 99

—Jerilyn Ross, quoted in "Gephyrophobia: A Fear of Crossing Bridges," CBS News, August 10, 2007. www.cbsnews.com.

Ross is a Washington, D.C.–based psychologist and president of the Anxiety Disorders Association of America.

66 We're justified in having this fear. Life was stressful before 9-11. It's gotten progressively worse. 99

—Herbert Benson, quoted in Claudia Kalb, "Coping with Anxiety," *Newsweek,* February 24, 2003, p. 51.

Benson is president of the Mind/Body Medical Institute of Boston, Massachusetts.

* Editor's Note: While the definition of a primary source can be narrowly or broadly defined, for the purposes of Compact Research, a primary source consists of: 1) results of original research presented by an organization or researcher; 2) eyewitness accounts of events, personal experience, or work experience; 3) first-person editorials offering pundits' opinions; 4) government officials presenting political plans and/or policies; 5) representatives of organizations presenting testimony or policy.

66 **Worrying about terrorists, war, a lousy economy and losing your job is not a disease. It's normal.** 99

—Arthur Kaplan, quoted in Karen Springen, "Taking the Worry Cure," *Newsweek,* February 24, 2003, p. 52.

Kaplan is a medical ethicist at the University of Pennsylvania in Philadelphia.

....

66 **People with [BII] phobias may faint at the scene of an accident or even at the sight of a syringe or needle. These are the only phobias associated with fainting.** 99

—Helen Saul, *Phobias: Fighting the Fear.* New York: Arcade, 2001, p. 49.

Saul is a medical and science journalist based in Great Britain and author of the book *Phobias: Fighting the Fear.*

....

66 **Not only will I not drive on highways, for the most part, but . . . if I am called on to drive anywhere new, I am in the absurd position of having to rehearse the drive first to see if I can handle it.** 99

—Allen Shawn, *Wish I Could Be There: Notes from a Phobic Life.* New York: Viking, 2007, pp. 125–26.

Shawn, a writer, musician, and composer, suffers from social and specific phobias and is the author of *Wish I Could Be There: Notes from a Phobic Life.*

....

❝[Social phobia] also exerts a powerful influence on the selection of a career. Thus, careers such as law or teaching are less appealing than computer science or other disciplines that involve communication with machines rather than people.❞

—Richard Restak, *Poe's Heart and the Mountain Climber: Exploring the Effect of Anxiety on Our Brains and Our Culture.* New York: Harmony, 2004, p. 156.

Restak is professor of neurology at George Washington University Medical Center in Washington, D.C., and author of the book *Poe's Heart and the Mountain Climber: Exploring the Effect of Anxiety on Our Brains and Our Culture.*

❝Alcohol can increase anxiety and even precipitate panic attacks. People with anxiety may drink to reduce anxiety, but down the road alcohol takes over and creates even more anxiety.❞

—Carolyn Chambers Clark, *Living Well with Anxiety.* New York: HarperCollins, 2006, p. 89.

Clark is a health educator and author of the book *Living Well with Anxiety.*

❝The classic formation of a phobia is when someone had a dramatic experience. And you don't have to be crossing a bridge when it collapses to have a bridge phobia.❞

— Seymour Segnit, quoted in Dan Childs and Katharine Stoel Gammon, "Minneapolis Disaster May Spark 'Bridge Phobia,'" ABC News, August 2, 2007. http://abcnews.go.com.

Segnit is president of Change That's Right Now Inc., a New York–based treatment center for phobia sufferers.

"We'd have a party on a Friday, and on the Monday before, I'd start sweating what I was going to say. I'd think about it in class and lie awake at night searching for anything. And that was with four days to go."

—Troy McKinley, quoted in Gerry Gropp, "Anxious Moments," *Golf World,* March 28, 2003, p. 28.

McKinley, a graduate of the University of the Pacific in Stockton, California, is a professional golfer and social phobia sufferer.

....

"About 20 percent of people treated for alcohol disorders and 30 percent of those with panic attacks also have social [phobia]. Depression, alcoholism, and panic attacks usually appear after social [phobia] and may be the result of it."

—Michael Craig Miller, ed., "Beyond Shyness and Stage Fright: Social Anxiety Disorder," *Harvard Mental Health Letter,* October 2003, p. 2.

Harvard Mental Health Letter is a professional journal published by the department of psychiatry at the Harvard University Medical School in Cambridge, Massachusetts.

....

"When asked whether they thought a lot about death, felt like they wanted to die, or felt so low they wanted to commit suicide, individuals with social phobia were more likely to say yes than individuals without social phobia."

—Richard G. Heimberg and Robert E. Becker, *Cognitive-Behavioral Group Therapy: Basic Mechanisms.* New York: Guilford, 2002, p. 44.

Heimberg is a professor of clinical psychology at Temple University in Philadelphia; Becker is a Philadelphia psychologist.

....

66 **People usually feel ashamed of their health-care pho- bia. They might never go to the doctor or the dentist or talk about it. But there is an obvious danger to not getting medical treatment. Avoiding medical treat- ment can be life-threatening.** 99

—Ellen Rodino, quoted in Melissa Dittmann, "When Health Fears Hurt Health," *Monitor on Psychology,* July/August 2005, p. 100.

Rodino is a psychologist who practices in Santa Monica, California.

66 **He didn't believe germs could come from him, just from the outside. He was convinced that he was going to be contaminated from the outside.** 99

—Raymond D. Fowler, quoted in Melissa Dittmann, "Hughes's Germ Phobia Revealed in Psychological Autopsy," *Monitor on Psychology,* July/August 2005, p. 102.

Fowler, a psychologist, was called on to provide a psychological evaluation of Howard Hughes following the billionaire's death in 1976; Hughes, who harbored a fear of germs, spent the last years of his life locked behind closed doors in a Las Vegas penthouse.

How Do Phobias Affect People?

- *Prevention* magazine reported in 2007 that **3.5 million** people have refused a medically necessary blood test or injection because they harbor **blood-injection-injury**, or BII, phobias.

- A Harvard University Medical School study concluded that the annual cost to the U.S. economy caused by anxiety disorders is **$42 billion**, CNN reported in 2007. About **$23 billion** of that amount was spent on nonpsychiatric medical treatment.

- A study conducted in Sweden found that **66 percent** of people who suffer from BII phobias have relatives who also harbor BII fears, author Helen Saul reports in her book *Phobias: Fighting the Fear*. Also, the Swedish study said, as many as **70 percent** of people who faint at the sight of blood have relatives who also faint when they see blood.

- A study reported in the psychiatric journal *Anxiety Annual Report* in 2001 found that **12 percent** of people with social phobia have attempted suicide at some point in their lives.

- The scientific journal *Harvard Mental Health Letter* reported in 2003 that adults who suffer from social phobia are **seven times** more likely than others to become depressed and twice as likely to **abuse alcohol**.

- Social phobia may form in children **as early as age 2**; a study published by the *Harvard Mental Health Letter* in 2003 said that **40 percent** of children who were considered shy at that age were still showing fear of others **at the age of 4**.

* According to a report published in 2007 in the *International Herald Tribune*, **15 percent** of American children suffer from social phobia; during the 1990s social phobia became the **third most common mental illness** in the United States, behind only depression and alcoholism.

Phobias Cause People to Miss Work

Social phobia and agoraphobia are among the major reasons people take time off from work. Statistics released in 2007 show that mental illness caused Americans to miss more than 1 billion days of work a year. People who suffer from social phobia miss 214 million days a year, while agoraphobes miss 37 million days a year.

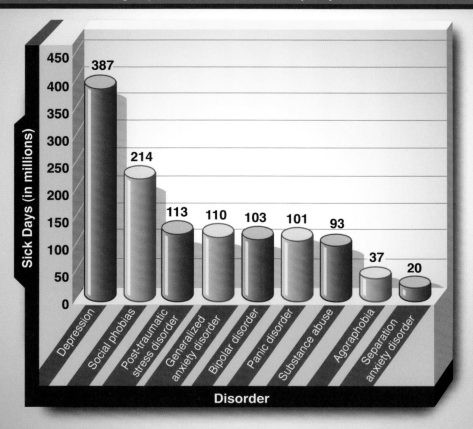

Source: Denise Gellen, "1 Billion Mental Health Days; Disorders Like Anxiety and Depression Top the List of Work Absences, a Study Says," *Los Angeles Times*, October 2, 2007.

- According to the journal *Monitor on Psychology*, people who harbor **BII phobias** often suffer from **obsessive-compulsive disorder**—they may wash their hands constantly—because they have convinced themselves that if they can avoid germs they do not have to see a doctor.

Reduced Opportunities for People with Social Phobia

A study performed by Dean Health Plan, an American insurance company, concluded that people who suffer from social phobia dramatically reduce their opportunities in life: They have a 10 percent lower probability of finishing college than others, and a 14 percent lower probability of finding jobs that require technical or managerial skills. Also, their wages are 10 percent lower than people who do not suffer from social phobia.

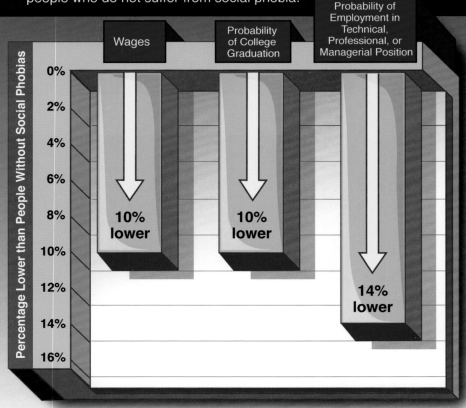

Source: David J. Katzelnick et al., "Impact of Generalized Social Anxiety Disorder in Managed Care," *American Journal of Psychiatry*, December 2001.

Social Phobia, Alcohol, and Suicide

Social phobia can be a high risk disease. Statistics compiled in 2001 show that people who suffer from social phobia are six times more likely to entertain thoughts of suicide than others. Also, social phobia patients are more than twice as likely as others to abuse alcohol. Some sufferers see substance abuse as a possible coping mechanism.

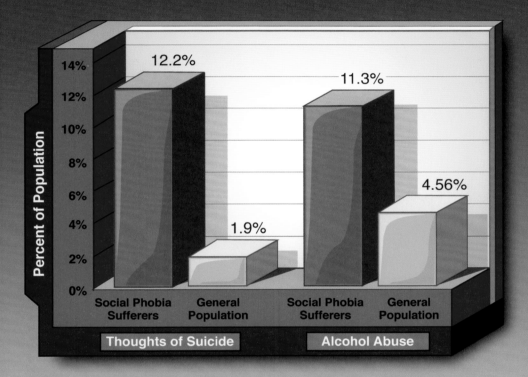

Sources: David J. Katzelnick et al., "Impact of Generalized Social Anxiety Disorder in Managed Care," *American Journal of Psychiatry,* December 2001; National Institute on Alcohol Abuse and Alcoholism, www.niaaa.nih.gov.

- A University of California at San Francisco study found that more than **50 percent of multiple sclerosis patients suffer from BII phobias** and cannot inject themselves with their medications, a particularly troubling trend because MS patients need daily injections of drugs to help them control their muscle spasms, the journal *Monitor on Psychology* reported in 2005.

Phobias Put a Strain on Health Care

The Dean Health Plan study found that patients who suffer from social phobia spend more time visiting their doctors than people who do not suffer from the illness. Those visits aren't necessarily to address the patients' mental health issues—people with social phobia suffer from an abundance of aches, pains, and other physical ailments. Also, the study said that social phobia patients pay more for their health care than others.

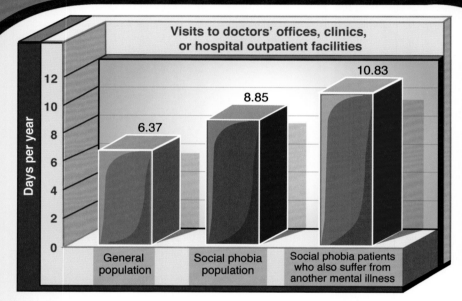

Visits to doctors' offices, clinics, or hospital outpatient facilities

Days per year

- General population: 6.37
- Social phobia population: 8.85
- Social phobia patients who also suffer from another mental illness: 10.83

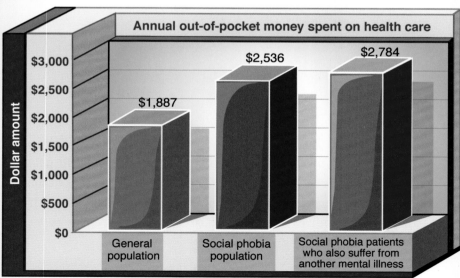

Annual out-of-pocket money spent on health care

Dollar amount

- General population: $1,887
- Social phobia population: $2,536
- Social phobia patients who also suffer from another mental illness: $2,784

Source: David J. Katzelnick et al., "Impact of Generalized Social Anxiety Disorder in Managed Care," *American Journal of Psychiatry*, December 2001.

Physical Reactions to Phobias

When the brain senses fear, it kick-starts the "fight or flight" reaction in the body: The lungs draw heavier breaths; the heart beats faster, sending more blood to the arms and legs; the liver releases sugar, providing more energy; and other changes occur that prepare the body for the physical stress of fighting or running away. People confronted with their phobia may experience these biological reactions.

Breathing
quickens to take in more oxygen

Heart
beats faster

Blood Pressure
rises

Liver
releases sugar into blood for added energy

Stomach
vessels constrict to force blood elsewhere

Perspiration
increases to regulate body temperature

Arms and Legs
receive extra blood for energy

- America's **15 million social phobics each miss 14 days** of work per person each year, according to statistics published in 2008 by the journal *New England Psychologist*.

- Author Richard Restak reports in his book *Poe's Heart and the Mountain Climber: Exploring the Effect of Anxiety on Our Brains and Our Culture* that people whose parents or other close relatives suffer from social phobia have a **16 percent** chance of also suffering from social phobia; people who do not have relatives suffering from social phobia have just a **5 percent** chance of developing the fear.

- A 2008 study by the Institute of Psychiatry in London, England, found that **15 percent** of adults faint while donating blood. The study also reported that **30 percent** of children are afraid of the sight of blood.

- Great Britain has so many belonephobes—**10 percent** of the population fears needles—that drug companies are developing other ways to deliver flu vaccines, such as through inhalers, the BBC reported in 2008.

- A 2003 report by the *Journal of the American Dental Association* said **63 percent** of adults reported feeling less pain during a dental visit than they recalled as children. The study suggested that dentists are using less painful techniques and are doing a better job of calming their patients' fears.

Can People Overcome Phobias?

> **One of the hardest things about having an anxiety disorder is that you feel so embarrassed and alone. When someone can say to you, 'I understand, I've been there,' it's a tremendous relief.**
>
> —Jerilyn Ross, president of the Anxiety Disorders Association of America.

The old story of Chicken Little says a lot about the danger of phobias. According to the fable, Chicken Little is eating her lunch one day when she is suddenly struck on the head by an acorn. Thinking that the sky is falling, Chicken Little panics and decides she must inform the king. As she makes her way to the king's castle, Chicken Little meets her friends Henny Penny, Goosey Loosey, and Turkey Lurkey and convinces them all that the sky is falling.

By now, everyone in the group has joined Chicken Little in her panic. Together, they set off in search of the king but soon encounter Foxy Loxy. Unlike the others, Foxy Loxy does not panic and, instead, turns the situation to his advantage. He leads them into his lair, where he gobbles up everyone.

The story of Chicken Little illustrates how phobias can dominate people's lives and eventually lead to their doom—so paralyzed by their fear that the sky is falling, Chicken Little and her friends neglect to recognize the real danger: a hungry fox. In the real world, nobody has to suffer the same fate as Chicken Little. Thanks to the science of psychiatry, drug treatment, and other therapies, phobias do not have to lead anyone toward their own doom.

As for Chicken Little's phobia, the fear of a falling sky has yet to be recorded as an actual specific phobia—although there are phobias that come close: meteorophobia, which is a fear of falling meteors, and uranophobia, fear of the heavens.

> **The story of Chicken Little illustrates how phobias can dominate people's lives and eventually lead to their doom.**

Just Relax

Some people can overcome their phobias simply by learning how to relax to reduce stress. Psychologists counsel people who suffer from phobias that the first step in overcoming their phobias is to realize their fears are irrational. Bethesda, Maryland, psychotherapist Jean Ratner, who specializes in working with people who are afraid to fly, counsels her patients to breathe deeply if they feel a panic attack coming on.

Ratner also advises patients to try to clear their heads of fearful thoughts—to concentrate on things other than their fears. "You can teach your brain not to run off with a frightening thought," she says. "It can be as simple as counting to eight, repetitively, over and over again."[37]

Meanwhile, people can reduce the stress in their lives in many ways. Many psychologists recommend exercise, yoga, and other physical activities. They also recommend that people try to keep family connections and friendships strong and to talk with family members and friends about their fears. Also, people should try to participate in activities that help make them feel good about themselves.

When Do People Seek Help?

At some point, though, people who suffer from phobias often realize they need professional help. But for some people who harbor specific phobias, that day may never come. They already lead full and active lives because they can easily avoid what frightens them, such as dogs or vacations aboard cruise ships.

But other types of phobias do get in the way of leading a full life. Business executives who travel a lot may find their careers quickly derailed if they harbor fears of flying, elevators, or tall buildings. As for

Advances in Neuroimaging

Meanwhile, science is pursuing other avenues. As physicians continue to study the brain itself and its role in fostering phobias, new techniques in imaging have given scientists a better look at the amygdalae and the other components of the brain. At New York University, medical researchers have tracked electrical impulses that travel to and from the amygdalae, and they have found that signals of danger travel faster to the amygdalae than impulses that carry other information. When the amygdalae perceive danger, they react by kick-starting the fight-or-flight response. Meanwhile, other components of the brain—the hippocampus and prefrontal cortex—take longer to react to danger.

All of this may occur within a few seconds or less, leading scientists to suspect that if the hippocampus and prefrontal cortex fail to suppress the fight-or-flight response, either they are reacting too slowly or the amygdalae are overreacting and creating a fight-or-flight response that the other components cannot control. The research indicates that in people who suffer from phobias, the amygdalae, hippocampus, and prefrontal cortex may not be operating in sync. Scientists do not know yet how to better synchronize them, but by recognizing the basic problem they may eventually be able to find a solution.

> As physicians continue to study the brain itself and its role in fostering phobias, new techniques in imaging have given scientists a better look at the amygdalae and the other components of the brain.

This type of research is likely to continue for many years. As scientists develop techniques to study the brain, new answers to the brain's mysteries are bound to surface. "This is a critical area of research for the future,"[45] Harvard Medical School psychiatrist Scott Rauch told the journal *Monitor on Psychology*.

Future Cures

In late 2007 Japanese scientists announced they had genetically altered the brain cells of some laboratory mice, removing the rodents' fears of cats. By tinkering with the rodents' DNA, the scientists were able to alter the mice's sense of smell, turning off certain nerve cells that alerted the mice to danger. In fact, mice use another sense to detect fear—the sense of hearing. As part of the experiment, the scientists did not alter the rodents' abilities to hear.

And so when the mice used their noses to smell the cats, they did not detect danger. But when the mice heard the cats' meows, they suddenly froze in terror. Therefore, the mice did not lose their ability to fear—only one of the genetic triggers of their fear. "This observation may suggest that the . . . mice only lacked the innate fear responses to cats' odors, but they did not lose the feeling of fear,"[46] the lead scientist in the study, Ko Kobayakawa, told the *London Telegraph*.

The Japanese scientists wondered whether the techniques could one day be applied to humans. "We think it has the power to clarify many unrevealed principles of the brain, those which generate emotions and behaviors,"[47] Kobayakawa told the *Telegraph*.

Certainly, tinkering with someone's DNA to wipe out fears of spiders or tall buildings may be a radical step, but the Japanese experiment does show that new information about how the brain responds to fear is surfacing all the time. Indeed, if science can find a way to block a mouse's true fear of being gobbled up by a cat, a cure for imaginary fears seems likely as well.

Primary Source Quotes*

Can People Overcome Phobias?

"People's fears are usually allayed when they feel like they have some control. Information gives people a sense of control of their destiny."

—Jerilyn Ross, quoted in Jennifer Huget, "Getting Over It," *Washington Post*, August 14, 2007, p. HE-1.

Ross is a Washington, D.C.–based psychologist and president of the Anxiety Disorders Association of America.

"The important thing to remember is that virtual reality is a tool in cognitive-behavioral therapy. It's not the answer in and of itself."

—Keith Saylor, quoted in Lea Winerman, "A Virtual Cure," *Monitor on Psychology*, July/August 2005, p. 87.

Saylor is a Washington, D.C.–based psychologist who specializes in treating patients with phobias.

* Editor's Note: While the definition of a primary source can be narrowly or broadly defined, for the purposes of Compact Research, a primary source consists of: 1) results of original research presented by an organization or researcher; 2) eyewitness accounts of events, personal experience, or work experience; 3) first-person editorials offering pundits' opinions; 4) government officials presenting political plans and/or policies; 5) representatives of organizations presenting testimony or policy.

"If the child is able to understand the importance of facing and confronting the dog or other phobic object, if they continue to gain positive experiences, the probability of relapsing is low."

—Wendy Silverman, quoted in Sadie F. Dingfelder, "Fighting Children's Fears, Fast," *Monitor on Psychology*, July/August 2005, p. 90.

Silverman is director of the Child Anxiety and Phobia Program at Florida International University.

"Not everyone with a known phobia actually gets treatment. But for those who do, symptoms can be controlled or disappear. They can function very well."

— Carlyle Chan, quoted in Lisa Jones Townsel, "When Fear Becomes Phobias, a Wicked Web Is Spun," *Milwaukee Journal Sentinel,* October 30, 2007. www.jsonline.com.

Chan is a professor of psychology at the Medical College of Wisconsin.

"They start going into social situations that have made them tense a thousand times before, but the trick now is that they are doing it with coping skills that will help them turn defeat into victory."

—Richard G. Heimberg, quoted in Melissa Dittmann, "Stemming Social Phobia," *Monitor on Psychology*, July/August 2005, p. 92.

Heimberg is a professor of clinical psychology at Temple University in Philadelphia.

❝I figured the more I did it [bungee jumping], the easier it would get.❞

—Craig Richards, quoted in Lisa Jones Townsel, "When Fear Becomes Phobias, a Wicked Web Is Spun," *Milwaukee Journal Sentinel*, October 30, 2007. www.jsonline.com.

Richards, 23, of Wisconsin Dells, Wisconsin, conquered his fear of heights by bungee jumping; he has now bungee jumped more than 400 times.

❝As individuals we are not the mere sum of our perceptions, fear memories, thoughts and emotions, but . . . something more. This is the big problem brain research needs to solve—how our brains make us who we are.❞

—Joseph LeDoux, quoted in Michael Behar, "Paging Dr. Fear," *Popular Science,* January 2008, p. 50.

LeDoux is a neuroscientist at New York University.

❝I felt at least a dawning awareness, in my fifties, that it might be possible for me to come to terms with some of the experiences I had avoided.❞

—Allen Shawn, *Wish I Could Be There: Notes from a Phobic Life.* New York: Viking, 2007, pp. 227–28.

Shawn, a writer, musician, and composer, suffers from social and specific phobias and is the author of *Wish I Could Be There: Notes from a Phobic Life.*

❝The first time, you might get the person relaxed and show them a toy or a cartoon image of the object. The next time, you might show them a film and then the third time you might ask them to touch the object. This way, phobias can normally be treated with about three hours of therapy.❞

—Felix Economakis, quoted in Lucy Elkins, "How I Overcame My Fish Phobia," *Daily Mail,* April 17, 2007. www.dailymail.co.uk.

Economakis is a British psychologist and frequent guest on the BBC television program *The Panic Room,* which explores phobias.

❝The capacity to relax is at the very foundation of any program undertaken to overcome anxiety, phobias, or panic attack.❞

—Edmund J. Bourne, *The Anxiety and Phobia Workbook.* Oakland, CA: New Harbinger, 2005, p. 74.

Bourne is a Kona, Hawaii–based psychologist who specializes in treatment of anxiety disorders and is author of the book *The Anxiety and Phobia Workbook.*

❝The good news about travel phobias is that they are treatable with cognitive-behavioral therapy, which helps patients recognize harmful patterns of thinking and behaving, and replaces them with healthier ones. Since the core problem in phobias is a set of false beliefs about the feared object or situation, the solution is to correct these wrong ideas and thereby remove the anxiety.❞

—Richard A. Friedman, " For Fearful Flyers, a Guide to Easing the Jitters," New York Times, Sept 18, 2006, p. F-11.

Friedman is professor of psychiatry at Weill Cornell Medical College, New York.

66 Looking back, I know my night fears were in my head. Imagined. I was simply afraid that 'something' would 'get' me but I had no idea what it might be. Franklin Roosevelt once said, '. . . the only thing we have to fear is fear itself . . .' and that describes my fear of the dark. 99

—Dwight Schuh, "Night Things," *Bowhunter*, May/June 2007, p. 80.

Schuh is an outdoors writer who overcame his nyctophobia, or fear of the dark, to become a successful bow hunter.

Facts and Illustrations

Can People Overcome Phobias?

- The journal *Harvard Mental Health Letter* reported the results of a survey in 2003 in which only **5 percent** of people suffering from social phobia said they had sought professional help.

- The **neurotransmitter oxytocin**, which controls the emotion of trust, has been found to **soothe the amygdalae**, the National Institute of Mental Health reported in 2005. Scientists believe that by boosting the brain's production of oxytocin, people would be less likely to develop phobias.

- A University of Wisconsin–Madison study found that people who **meditated six days a week for eight weeks** used more rationale when confronted by fears; they also had lower anxiety and less activity in their amygdalae, *Newsweek* reported in 2003.

- University of Wyoming psychologist Brett Deacon told *Prevention* in 2007 that he advises his blood-injection-injury phobia patients to **sing or hum** when a physician or nurse approaches them with a needle.

- In a 2005 University of Quebec study, **six of the 11** arachnophobes who were given cognitive-behavioral therapy through virtual reality were able to stand next to a glass bowl containing a spider at the conclusion of the therapy; four participants could **touch the spider** with a pencil.

Confronting Fear Helps People with Arachnophobia

In a study at the University of Washington, two groups of arachnophobes were given cognitive-behavioral therapy through virtual reality. In the test, the members of one group were asked to touch a virtual reality spider which was, of course, not really there. The others were asked to do the same task, but when they reached out to touch the spider they actually touched a realistic model of a spider. After the treatment, the arachnophobes who touched the model were able to draw themselves much closer to a real spider than those who touched the imaginary spider.

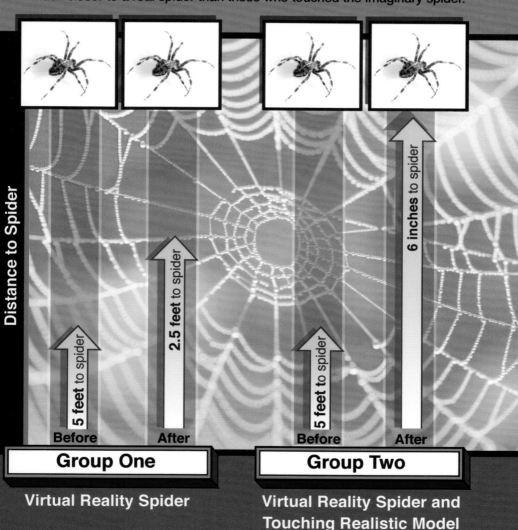

Distance to Spider

5 feet to spider — Before

2.5 feet to spider — After

Group One

Virtual Reality Spider

5 feet to spider — Before

6 inches to spider — After

Group Two

Virtual Reality Spider and Touching Realistic Model

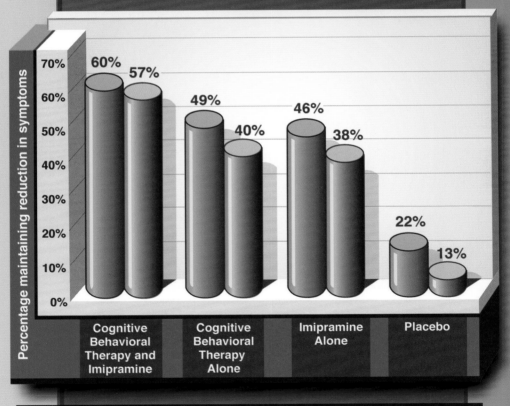

Panic Attacks Caused by Phobias Are Treatable with Therapy and Medication

A Boston University study looked at the effectiveness of antidepressant drugs and cognitive-behavioral therapy in conquering panic attacks caused by phobias and other anxiety disorders. A total of 312 patients were split into four groups. The first group was treated with cognitive-behavioral therapy; the second group was treated with Imipramine, an antidepressant drug; the third group was given both; and the fourth group was given a placebo. Group members given cognitive-behavioral therapy and the drug had the most success in controlling their panic symptoms during the two phases of the test.

Percentage maintaining reduction in symptoms

| | 60% | 57% | 49% | 40% | 46% | 38% | 22% | 13% |

Cognitive Behavioral Therapy and Imipramine · Cognitive Behavioral Therapy Alone · Imipramine Alone · Placebo

Patients maintaining reduction in symptoms in first 12 weeks of treatment

Patients maintaining reduction in symptoms for next 26 weeks

Source: David H. Barlow et al., "Cognitive-Behavioral Therapy, Imipramine, or Their Combination for Panic Disorder: A Randomized Controlled Trial," *Journal of the American Medical Association*, May 17, 2000.

Tuberculosis Drug Helps Reduce Phobias

Mental health researchers at New York University have experimented with the antibiotic drug d-cycloserine, or DCS, which is used to treat tuberculosis. A positive side-effect of the drug is improved memory, so when the eyes send a new image to the visual cortex, the drug responds by sending a new memory to the amygdala. For people who suffer from phobias, DCS may help them replace their old fearful memories with newer and less-fearful memories.

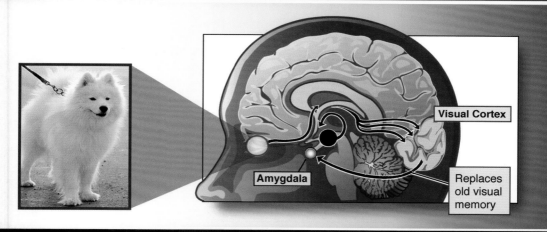

Source: Michael Behar, "Paging Dr. Fear," *Popular Science*, January 2008.

- According to the journal *Monitor on Psychology*, studies show that **80 percent** of social phobics can ease their fears through a combination of cognitive-behavioral therapy and antidepressant drugs, and most remain symptom-free for at least five years.

- Certain **herbs and dietary supplements** may help ease the symptoms of anxiety disorders, including social and specific phobias, the journal *Harvard Women's Health Watch* reported in 2007. Among the herbs and supplements found to have **antianxiety qualities** are kava, which can be brewed in a tea; valerian and passion flower, which are herbs that act as sedatives; and inositol, a vitamin B supplement that inhibits serotonin.

Using Hormones to Fight Phobias

An increase in the hormone cortisol may help reduce phobias, according to a 2006 study performed at the University of Zurich in Switzerland. In the experiment, a group of people with social phobia was administered doses of cortisone, a drug produced in the body by cortisol. A second group of social phobia patients was given a placebo—they were told the drug would reduce their anxiety, but it contained no benefits. Ninety minutes after taking the drug, members of both groups were asked to give speeches in public—a situation that should cause fear in people with social phobia. Researchers created a "fear scale" and, based on their observations of the phobia sufferers during their speeches, rated each participant on a scale of one to six. The results show that phobia patients who ingested cortisone were clearly better able to control their fears than the patients who were given the placebos.

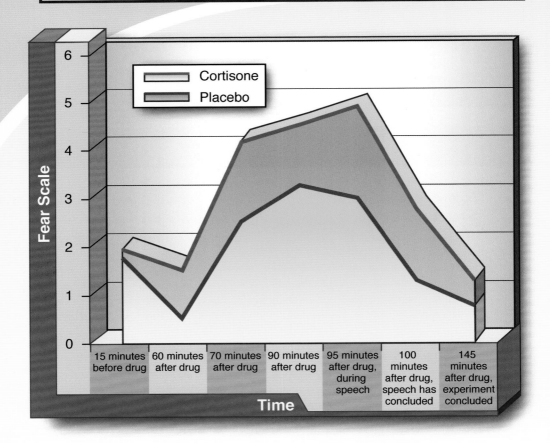

Source: Lelia M. Soravia et al., "Glucocorticoids Reduce Phobic Fear in Humans,"
PNAS, April 4, 2006. www.pnas.org.

- Psychologists working with the University of the Pacific School of Dentistry in San Francisco have found that **hypnosis helps** some patients get through their dental appointments; the hypnotic therapy helps the patients focus on other thoughts during their dental treatments, *Monitor on Psychology* reported in 2005.

- A study reported by *Monitor on Psychology* in 2005 urged family members to be more **considerate of agoraphobics**; the study found that symptoms of agoraphobia intensified in individuals when their family members were hostile and less understanding of the patients' problems.

- Drugs that put people to sleep in their dentists' offices have gone into widespread use in Canada, *Maclean's* reported in 2007. The increased use of the knockout drugs should not come as a shock, the magazine said, because a University of Toronto study found that **16 percent of Canadians** suffer from dentophobia.

- Researchers at the University of California at Berkeley have designed a **"pulsed microjet"** device that uses air pressure to deliver drugs into the body without the need of a needle; each year, it is estimated that medical professionals deliver **12 billion needle injections** to the world's population.

- The psychology department at Stockholm University in Sweden has established a cognitive-behavioral therapy program in which **80 to 95 percent** of participants get their phobias under control after just one session, *Time* reported in 2001.

Key People and Advocacy Groups

Air Travelers Association: The Air Travelers Association, based in Potomac, Maryland, is an advocacy group for people who travel frequently by air. People who suffer from aviophobia may be interested in some of the association's projects, which include providing reports on the world's safest airlines as well as assessments of the airlines' measures to provide comfort and services to passengers.

American Dental Association: The American Dental Association provides many resources for its members on steps they can take to alleviate the fears of their patients. Dentists are schooled in the latest advances in sedatives and painkillers as well as other techniques they can employ to help alleviate fear, such as providing full explanations of their procedures to their patients.

Albert Ellis: When Ellis, a New York psychotherapist, developed "rational therapy" in the 1950s, he believed it could be effective in treating a variety of mental illnesses. Now known as cognitive-behavioral therapy, the treatment involves introducing small doses of what causes anxiety in people so they may gradually adjust to fearful situations.

Sigmund Freud: After interviewing "Little Hans," a boy who was afraid of horses, the founder of modern psychoanalysis suggested that phobias are caused by sexual urges. Freud's theory was eventually discarded, but his ideas for treating phobic people have been followed for decades. Freud encouraged phobic people to talk about what frightens them.

Joseph LeDoux: A New York University neuroscientist, LeDoux is one of the country's leading experts in how the amygdalae affect people's reactions to fearful situations. LeDoux believes drug therapy can alter the amygdalae, replacing people's fearful memories with newer, less threatening memories.

National Emetophobia Society: The National Emetophobia Society provides information and support for people who harbor a fear of vomiting. Visitors to the society's Web site, www.emetophobia.org, can find coping techniques, discussion forums, lists of unusual behaviors members have taken to avoid vomiting, and even a list of vomit-inducing movies members are urged to avoid.

National Phobics' Society: The chief advocacy group for phobia sufferers in Great Britain, the National Phobics' Society helps link patients with therapists, produces numerous publications about phobias, and provides British phobics with a hotline to call when they are in need of help.

Jerilyn Ross: Ross overcame her own fear of tall buildings to break out of a dead-end career and establish a psychology practice in Washington, D.C., that specializes in treating phobic people. Ross has become a leading spokeswoman for phobia treatment. She serves as president of the Anxiety Disorders Association of America.

Society for Neuroscience: The Society for Neuroscience is the professional association of physicians and scientists who study the brain and seek physiological answers for mental illnesses. In addition to publishing professional journals and scheduling conferences for neuroscientists, the organization also provides information to the public on trends and new discoveries in neuroscience.

John B. Watson and Rosalie Raynor: By clanging a steel bar behind the head of a little boy named Albert B., Watson and Raynor established behaviorism as the cause of most phobias, proving that people's irrational fears are grounded in unpleasant experiences. Behaviorism is also regarded as the cause for other anxiety disorders, particularly post-traumatic stress disorder, which afflicts many veterans of warfare and victims of crime who experience a single horrific event or series of events in their lives.

Chronology

1920
After experimenting with a baby named Albert B., John B. Watson and Rosalie Raynor develop the theory of behaviorism, declaring that bad memories are the cause of phobias.

ca. 2500 B.C.
Greek physician Hippocrates first notes the symptoms of social phobia in a patient who refuses to leave home during the day; at night, the patient avoids contact with others.

1909
Sigmund Freud examines "Little Hans" and incorrectly deduces that sexual urges are at the root of the boy's fear of horses.

1805
The story of the arachnophobic Little Miss Muffet is first published as a nursery rhyme.

2500 B.C.   1750   1825   1900   1975

1893
Norwegian artist Edvard Munch paints *The Scream*, depicting human fear and anxiety.

1976
Eccentric billionaire Howard Hughes dies after spending the last 10 years of his life locked in a Las Vegas penthouse where he believed he could avoid contact with germs.

1953
Albert Ellis develops cognitive-behavioral therapy in which phobic people are exposed to their fears in small steps, helping them overcome what frightens them.

1979
Giving in to his fear of flying, football broadcaster John Madden starts touring the country in the "Madden Cruiser," an $800,000 tour bus that he uses to travel from game to game.

1980
The Phobia Society of America is established, providing phobia sufferers with an advocacy group as well as a source of information on their illnesses and how to seek therapy; later, the group changes its name to the Anxiety Disorders Association of America.

2000
The U.S. Food and Drug Administration endorses the antidepressant drug Paxil specifically for treatment of social phobia.

2001
The September 11 terrorist attacks spark a wave of aviophobia among Americans; in Europe, fear of Muslims, or Islamophobia, becomes a growing trend.

1999
Noted Welsh physician James Kidd dies of a drug overdose after losing his job; the medical examiner determines Kidd's intense fear of the dentist led to his suicide.

1985 **1990** **1995** **2000** **2005**

1987
Pop artist Andy Warhol dies from complications from an infected gallbladder; Warhol's fear of hospitals and his refusal to seek medical care until the last minute are likely to have contributed to his condition.

2006
The film *Snakes on a Plane*, which dramatized fear of flying and fear of snakes, earns more than $62 million at the box office.

1995
A team of researchers at Georgia Institute of Technology reports the effectiveness of virtual reality during cognitive-behavioral therapy treatments.

2007
Scientists in Japan remove a mouse's fear of cats by altering the rodent's DNA.

Related Organizations

American Psychiatric Association

1000 Wilson Blvd., Suite 1825
Arlington, VA 22209-3901
phone: (888) 357-7924
e-mail: apa@psych.org
Web site: www.psych.org

The organization serves as a professional association for some 38,000 American psychiatrists, who are physicians specializing in treating mental illnesses. Visitors to the association's Web site can find many resources about phobias and anxiety disorders as well as news about developments in psychiatric medicine.

American Psychological Association

750 First St. NE
Washington, DC 20002-4242
phone: (800) 374-2721
e-mail: public.affairs@apa.org
Web site: www.apa.org

The American Psychological Association represents more than 148,000 American psychologists, who are professionals who study and treat human behavior. Visitors to the association's Web site can access current and past issues of APA's magazine *Monitor on Psychology*, which has published many articles about phobias and anxiety disorders.

Anxiety Disorders Association of America

8730 Georgia Ave., Suite 600
Silver Spring, MD 20910
phone: (240) 485-1001
fax: (240) 485-1035
Web site: www.adaa.org

Founded in 1980, the organization promotes awareness about anxiety disorders by providing information to the public, media, government officials, mental health professionals, and others about the affliction. Visitors to the association's Web site can take a phobia test to determine whether their fears are irrational.

Anxiety Disorders Association of Canada

PO Box 117, Station Cote St-Luc
Montreal, Quebec H4V 2Y3
phone: (888) 223-2252
fax: (514) 484-7892
e-mail: contactus@anxietycanada.ca
Web site: www.anxietycanada.ca

The association is Canada's chief advocacy group for people who suffer from anxiety disorders. Visitors to the association's Web site can find an archive of news stories about trends in phobias and other anxiety disorders in Canada.

Association for Behavioral and Cognitive Therapies

305 7th Ave., 16th Floor
New York, NY 10001
phone: (212) 647-1890
fax: (212) 647-1865
Web site: www.aabt.org

The association represents therapists who provide cognitive-behavioral therapy for people who suffer from phobias and other anxiety disorders. Students who visit the association's Web site can find fact sheets on a long list of mental illnesses that may be treated by cognitive-behavioral therapy. In addition to phobias, other ailments that can be treated include bed-wetting, eating disorders, and drug abuse.

Center for Anxiety and Related Disorders at Boston University

648 Beacon St., 6th Floor, Kenmore Square
Boston, MA 02215

phone: (617) 353-9610

Web site: www.bu.edu/anxiety

The center provides treatment for people who suffer from phobias and other anxiety disorders and also performs research into the causes of anxiety disorders. Visitors to the center's Web site can read brief explanations of social phobia, specific phobia, and agoraphobia and read updates on the center's research activities.

Center for Neural Science

New York University

4 Washington Pl., Room 809

New York, NY 10003-6621

phone: (212) 998-7780

fax: (212) 995-4704

Web site: www.cns.nyu.edu/ledoux

New York University's Center for Neural Science performs cutting-edge research on how the amygdalae affect the body's reactions to fear. Visitors to the center's Web site can view the slide shows *Fear in the Age of Terror* and *Remembering Fear* and watch the video *Science, Music, and Your Brain*, which features an interview with the center's director, Joseph LeDoux.

Mental Health America

2000 N. Beauregard St, 6th Floor

Alexandria, VA 22311

phone: (800) 969-6642

fax: (703) 684-5968

Web site: www.nmha.org

Formerly the National Mental Health Association, Mental Health America is an advocacy group for people with mental illnesses as well as their families. The organization helps people with phobias and other anxiety disorders find support groups, therapists, and other sources of assistance.

National Alliance on Mental Illness

Colonial Place Three, 2107 Wilson Blvd., Suite 300
Arlington, VA 22201-3042
phone: (703) 524-7600
fax: (703) 524-9094
Web site: www.nami.org

The alliance is the chief advocacy group for people with mental illnesses and includes local chapters in every state. On the alliance's Web site, young people with concerns about mental illnesses can participate in online discussion forums about many topics, including phobias.

National Institute of Mental Health

6001 Executive Blvd.
Bethesda, MD 20892-9663
phone: (866) 615-6464
e-mail: nimhinfo@nih.gov
Web site: www.nimh.nih.gov

An agency of the National Institutes of Health, the National Institute of Mental Health is the federal government's chief funding agency for mental health research in America. Students can find many resources about phobias on the agency's Web site, including the publication *Anxiety Disorders*, which can be downloaded.

For Further Research

Books

Martin M. Antony and Mark A. Watling, *Overcoming Medical Phobias: How to Conquer Fear of Blood, Needles, Doctors, and Dentists.* Oakland, CA: New Harbinger, 2006.

Donald L. Barlett and James Steele, *Howard Hughes: His Life and Madness.* New York: W.W. Norton, 2004.

Edmund J. Bourne, *The Anxiety and Phobia Workbook.* Oakland, CA: New Harbinger, 2005.

Carolyn Chambers Clark, *Living Well with Anxiety.* New York: Harper-Collins, 2006.

Terry Cunningham, *The Hell of Social Phobia: One Man's 40 Year Struggle.* London: Stagedoor, 2005.

Howard Liebgold, *Freedom from Fear: Overcoming Anxiety, Phobias, and Panic.* New York: Citadel, 2004.

Reneau Z. Peurifoy, *Anxiety, Phobias, and Panic.* New York: Hachette USA, 2005.

Richard Restak, *Poe's Heart and the Mountain Climber: Exploring the Effect of Anxiety on Our Brains and Our Culture.* New York: Harmony, 2004.

Helen Saul, *Phobias: Fighting the Fear.* New York: Arcade, 2001.

Allen Shawn, *Wish I Could Be There: Notes from a Phobic Life.* New York: Viking, 2007.

Periodicals

Joelle Attinger, "All Aboard Exposure Airlines," *Time,* April 2, 2001.

Michael Behar, "Paging Dr. Fear," *Popular Science,* January 2008.

Geoffrey Cowley et al., "Our Bodies, Our Fears," *Newsweek,* February 24, 2003.

Jennifer Huget, "Getting Over It," *Washington Post*, August 14, 2007.

Imani Josey, "Studies Highlight Phobias Affecting Blacks; Possible Link to Neighborhoods," *Jet*, August 27, 2007.

Claudia Kalb, "Coping with Anxiety," *Newsweek*, February 24, 2003.

Jeffrey Kluger, Dan Cray, Brad Liston, and Ulla Plon, "Fear Not!" *Time*, April 2, 2001.

Kristyn Kusek, "Could a Fear Wreak Havoc on Your Life?" *Cosmopolitan*, May 2001.

Mike Lipton and Linda Trischitta, "Recipe for Living," *People*, August 22, 2005.

Nancy MacDonald, "The Root Canal of Your Dreams," *Maclean's*, December 17, 2007.

Leah Paulos, "Scared Silly," *Current Health 1*, October 2006.

Prevention, "Calm a Needling Fear," May 2007.

Nina M. Riccio, "Do You Suffer from High Anxiety?" *Current Health 2*, October 2003.

Mark Roth, "Born Scared? Why Do We Think Spiders and Snakes Are So Scary? It Just Might Be Evolution," *Pittsburgh Post-Gazette*, March 7, 2007.

Alyssa Shaffer, "Fear Not! Therapist Jerilyn Ross Offers Hope for Conquering Phobias," *Biography*, May 2001.

David M. Shribman, "Black Moods in the White House: Many Presidents Suffered from Mental Illness and yet They Were Highly Functional and Successful," *Pittsburgh Post-Gazette*, May 21, 2006.

Deborah Solomon, "A Gloom of Her Own," *New York Times Magazine*, November 21, 2004.

Karen Springen, "Taking the Worry Cure," *Newsweek*, February 24, 2003.

Andrew Staub, "Friday the 13th: Superstition or Phobia?" *Wilkes-Barre Citizens' Voice*, July 13, 2007.

Marianne Szegedy-Maszak, "Conquering Our Phobias," *U.S. News & World Report*, December 6, 2004.

Teen People, "What's Your Phobia?" September 2006.

Del Quentin Wilbur, "In a Brave New World, a Heightened Fear of Flying," *Washington Post*, January 6, 2007.

Internet Sources

Hollie McKay, "Fame-o-Phobia: What Scares the Stars?" Fox News, March 15, 2007. www.foxnews.com/story/0,2933,258643,00.html.

National Institute of Mental Health, "Anxiety Disorders," 2007. www.nimh.nih.gov/health/publications/anxiety-disorders/summary.shtml.

Joanne Cavanaugh Simpson, "It's All in the Upbringing," *Johns Hopkins Magazine*, April 2000. www.jhu.edu/~jhumag/0400web/35.html.

Natasha Stillwell, Discovery Channel–Canada, "Top Ten Phobias," March 22, 2004. www.exn.ca/Stories/2004/03/22/51.asp?t=dp.

Buck Wolf, "Wolf Files: Celebrity Phobias," ABC News, December 16, 2003. http://abcnews.go.com/Entertainment/WolfFiles/story?id=116591&page=1.

Source Notes

Overview

1. Richard Restak, *Poe's Heart and the Mountain Climber: Exploring the Effect of Anxiety on Our Brains and Our Culture.* New York: Harmony, 2004, p. 2.
2. Allen Shawn, *Wish I Could Be There: Notes from a Phobic Life.* New York: Viking, 2007, p. xviii.
3. Quoted in Buck Wolf, "Wolf Files: Celebrity Phobias," ABC News, December 16, 2003. http://abcnews.go.com.
4. Quoted in Marianne Szegedy-Maszak, "Conquering Our Phobias," *U.S. News & World Report*, December 6, 2004, p. 66.
5. David J. Katzelnick et al., "Impact of Generalized Social Anxiety Disorder in Managed Care," *American Journal of Psychiatry*, December 2001, p. 2006.
6. Quoted in Geoffrey Cowley et al., "Our Bodies, Our Fears," *Newsweek*, February 24, 2003, p. 42.
7. Quoted in Szegedy-Maszak, "Conquering Our Phobias," p. 66.
8. Quoted in Michele Snipe, "Psychologist Uses Virtual Reality to Curb Phobias," *Inside Fordham*, September 2003. www.fordham.edu.

What Are Phobias?

9. Carolyn Chambers Clark, *Living Well with Anxiety.* New York: HarperCollins, 2006, p. 2.
10. Reneau Z. Peurifoy, *Anxiety, Phobias, and Panic.* New York: Hachette USA, 2005, pp. 6–7.
11. Quoted in Jeffrey Kluger et al., "Fear Not!" *Time*, April 2, 2001, p. 52.
12. Quoted in *Teen People*, "What's Your Phobia?" September 2006, p. 37.
13. Quoted in Mike Lipton and Linda Trischitta, "Recipe for Living," *People*, August 22, 2005, p. 113.
14. Quoted in Lipton and Trischitta, "Recipe for Living," p. 113.
15. Restak, *Poe's Heart and the Mountain Climber*, p. 141.
16. Shawn, *Wish I Could Be There*, pp. xv–xvi.

What Causes Phobias?

17. Quoted in Helen Saul, *Phobias: Fighting the Fear.* New York: Arcade, 2001, p. 18.
18. Quoted in Saul, *Phobias: Fighting the Fear*, p. 18.
19. Quoted in Saul, *Phobias: Fighting the Fear*, p. 18.
20. Saul, *Phobias: Fighting the Fear*, p. 224.
21. Saul, *Phobias: Fighting the Fear*, p. 224.
22. Quoted in Stanley Rachman, *Anxiety.* London: Psychology Press, 2004, p. 72.
23. Quoted in Joanne Cavanaugh Simpson, "It's All in the Upbringing," *Johns Hopkins Magazine*, April 2000. www.jhu.edu.
24. Quoted in Szegedy-Maszak, "Conquering Our Phobias," p. 66.
25. Restak, *Poe's Heart and the Mountain Climber*, p. 209.
26. Saul, *Phobias: Fighting the Fear*, p. 56.

How Do Phobias Affect People?

27. Quoted in Kluger et al., "Fear Not!" p. 52.
28. Quoted in Melissa Dittman, "Stemming Social Phobia," *Monitor on Psychology*, July/August 2005, p. 92.
29. Katzelnick et al., "Impact of Generalized Social Anxiety Disorder in Managed Care," p. 2,005.

30. Timothy J. Bruce and Sy Atezaz Saeed, "Social Anxiety Disorder: A Common, Under-recognized Mental Disorder," *American Family Physician*, November 15, 1999. www.aafp.org.

31. Katzelnick et al., "Impact of Generalized Social Anxiety Disorder in Managed Care," p. 2,006.

32. Quoted in BBC News, "Shamed Doctor Killed Himself," July 20, 2000. http://news.bbc.co.uk.

33. Quoted in BBC News, "Shamed Doctor Killed Himself."

34. Quoted in Bob Colacello, *Holy Terror: Andy Warhol Close Up*. New York: HarperCollins, 1990, p. 489.

35. Quoted in Dan Childs and Katharine Stoel Gammon, "Minneapolis Disaster May Spark 'Bridge Phobia,'" ABC News, August 2, 2007. http://abcnews.go.com.

36. Quoted in CBS News, "Gephyrophobia: A Fear of Crossing Bridges," August 10, 2007. www.cbsnews.com.

Can People Overcome Phobias?

37. Quoted in Jennifer Huget, "Getting Over It," *Washington Post*, August 14, 2007, p. HE-1.

38. Quoted in Lynne L. Hall, "Fighting Phobias: The Things That Go Bump in the Night," *FDA Consumer*, March 1997. www.fda.gov.

39. Jerilyn Ross, "About Jerilyn Ross," Ross Center for Anxiety and Related Disorders. www.rosscenter.com.

40. Joelle Attinger, "All Aboard Exposure Airlines," *Time*, April 2, 2001, p. 52.

41. Attinger, "All Aboard Exposure Airlines," p. 52.

42. Quoted in Attinger, "All Aboard Exposure Airlines," p. 52.

43. Attinger, "All Aboard Exposure Airlines," p. 52.

44. Quoted in Candace Murphy, "10 Terrors: Phobias Disrupt Daily Life," *San Jose Mercury News*, December 19, 2003.

45. Quoted in Lea Winerman, "Figuring Out Phobia," *Monitor on Psychology*, July/August 2005, p. 96.

46. Quoted in Roger Highfield, "Cat-and-Mouse Game Driven by Sense of Fear," *London Telegraph*, November 7, 2007. www.telegraph.co.uk.

47. Quoted in Highfield, "Cat-and-Mouse Game Driven by Sense of Fear."

List of Illustrations

What Are Phobias?
Phobias Most Common Type of Anxiety Disorder   33
Anxiety Among College Students May Lead to Agoraphobia   34
Americans Fear Snakes the Most   35

What Causes Phobias?
Response to Fear   50
Memories and Phobias   51
How the Body Processes Fear   52
Phobias Caused by Out of Sync Brain   53

How Do Phobias Affect People?
Phobias Cause People to Miss Work   69
Reduced Opportunities for People with Social Phobia   70
Social Phobia, Alcohol, and Suicide   71
Phobias Put a Strain on Health Care   72
Physical Reactions to Phobias   73

Can People Overcome Phobias?
Confronting Fear Helps People with Arachnophobia   89
Panic Attacks Caused by Phobias Are Treatable with Therapy
    and Medication   90
Tuberculosis Drug Helps Reduce Phobias   91
Using Hormones to Fight Phobias   92

List of Illustrations

Index

acrophobia (fear of heights), 23
agoraphobia (fear of marketplace),
    23–24
    among African Americans, 36
    treatment for, 87
agyrophobia (fear of crossing street),
    23
Albert B, 40, 44
alcohol
    anxiety and, 65
    social phobias and abuse of, 68, 71
        (chart)
Amaral, David, 45
American Family Physician (journal),
    32, 57
American Journal of Psychiatry, 16
amygdala, 7, 13, 40–41, 47, 50
    (illustration)
time for transmission of fear signals to
    rest of body from, 49
antidepressants, 17, 80
Anxiety, Phobias, and Panic (Peurifoy),
    22
Anxiety Annual Report (journal), 68
anxiety disorders, 9, 19
    annual cost of, 68
    generalized, 20
    prevalence of, 8
        by type, 33 (chart)
    types of, 19
arachnophobia, 10
arachnophobia (fear of spiders), 36
    cognitive-behavioral/virtual reality
        therapy for, 88
Archer, Carolyn, 30
Attinger, Joelle, 79
auditory thalamus, 49
aviophobia (fear of flying), 23

Ayers, Elise, 62

Barlow, David H., 17, 90
Becker, Robert E., 66
Beckham, David, 14
Beckham, Victoria, 14
Behar, Michael, 48, 91
Behavioral and Cognitive Psychotherapy
    (journal), 36
behaviorism, 40
belonephobia (fear of needles), 74
Benson, Herbert, 63
blood-injection-injury (BII) phobia,
    23, 60
    among multiple sclerosis patients,
        71
    fainting and, 64
    obsessive-compulsive disorder and,
        70
    refusal of care based on, 68
Bourne, Edmund J., 86
brain
    abnormalities in, 13
    imaging of, 81
    mechanism of fear response in, 50
        (illustration), 51 (illustration), 52
        (illustration), 53 (illustration)
    parts involved in development of
        phobias, 40–41
    See also amygdala; hippocampus;
        prefrontal cortex
Brennan, Gareth, 31
bridges, fear of. *See* gephyrophobia

caffeine, 54
Chan, Carlyle, 29, 84
Chicken Little, 75–76
children, fear of clowns among, 32

chrometophobia (fear of money), 32
Clark, Carolyn Chambers, 19, 47, 65
claustrophobia (fear of confined
   spaces), 23
cognitive-behavioral therapy, 17,
   77–78, 83
   with antidepressants, for social
      phobia, 90 (chart)
   for arachnophobia, 88, 89
      (illustration)
   computer technology and, 18
   for panic attacks, vs. drug therapy,
      90 (chart)
   success of, 93
Colacello, Bob, 60
Coolidge, Calvin, 36
cortisone, 80
   in treatment of phobias, 92 (chart)
Cosmopolitan (magazine), 54
Cox, Beth, 14–15, 17
Craske, Michelle, 23, 46
crossing street, fear of. See
   agyrophobia

Damocles, 37
d-cycloserine (DCS), 91
de Montaigne, Michel, 46
Deacon, Brett, 88
Deen, Paula, 24
dentophobia (fear of dentists), 59
   prevalence of, 93
Depp, Johnny, 28
dopamine, 42
drug therapy, 80
   with cognitive-behavioral therapy,
      for social phobia, 91
   for panic attacks, vs. cognitive-
      behavioral therapy, 90 (chart)

Economakis, Felix, 48, 86
Edwards, Ian, 59
Ellis, Albert, 77–78
emetophobia (fear of vomiting), 36

enclosed places, fear of. See
   claustrophobia

fear, as normal emotion, 20–21
fight-or-flight response, 21–22, 73
   (illustration)
flying, fear of. See aviophobia
Foa, Edna B., 46
Fowler, Raymond D., 67
Freud, Sigmund, 37, 39
Friday the thirteenth, fear of. See
   paraskevidekatriaphobia
Friedman, Richard A., 86

generalized anxiety disorder (GAD),
   20
gephyrophobia (fear of bridges),
   61–62
glossophobia (fear of public speaking),
   35

Harvard Mental Health Letter
   (journal), 68, 88
Harvard Women's Health Watch, 91
heights, fear of. See acrophobia
Heimberg, Richard G., 55, 56, 66, 84
herbs/dietary supplements, 91
Hilfer, Alan, 61
hippocampus, 41, 51 (illustration)
   social phobias and, 54
Hippocrates, 37–38
hospitals, fear of. See nosocomephobia
Hsia, Curtis, 79
Hughes, Howard, 14, 67
hypnosis, during dental treatments, 93

Inside Fordham (journal), 18
International Herald Tribune
   (newspaper), 69
intruders, fear of. See scelerophobia
Islamophobia (fear of Muslims), 36

Jackson, Sheryl, 77
Jefferson, Thomas, 36
Jelinek, Elfriede, 27

Johnson, Lyndon B., 36
Journal of Clinical Psychiatry, 41
Journal of Neuroscience, 52
Journal of the American Dental Association, 74

Kaplan, Arthur, 64
Kidd, James, 59
Kirsch, Barbara, 80
Kobayakawa, Ko, 82

LeDoux, Joseph, 41, 44, 85
Little Hans, 39–40, 47
Liu, Benjamin, 60
Living Well with Anxiety (Clark), 19
London Telegraph (newspaper), 82

Maclean's (magazine), 93
Madden, John, 13–14
marketplace, fear of. *See* agoraphobia
Marsden, James, 28
Matthews, Dave, 28
McGaugh, James, 47
McKay, Dean, 18
McKinley, Troy, 66
meteorophobia (fear of meteors), 76
Miller, Michael Craig, 66
money, fear of. *See* chrometophobia
Monitor on Psychology (journal), 56, 70, 71, 81, 91, 93

National Institute of Mental Health (NIH), 43, 88
on prevalence of anxiety disorders, 8
Nature (journal), 49
Nature Neuroscience (journal), 53
needles, fear of. *See* belonephobia
neuroimaging, 81
neurotransmitters, 13
abnormalities with, 41–42
antidepressants and, 17
New England Psychologist (journal), 74
Newsweek (magazine), 49, 50, 88

norepinephrine, 42
nosocomephobia (fear of hospitals), 60

obsessive-compulsive disorder, 70
O'Connell, Caileigh, 29
ombrophobia (fear of rain), 42–43
ophidiophobia (fear of snakes), 35
oxytocin, 88

Panettiere, Hayden, 23
panic attacks, 7, 15, 24
cognitive-behavioral vs. drug therapy for, 90 (chart)
symptoms of, 24
panic disorder, 20
paraskevidekatriaphobia (fear of Friday the thirteenth), 36
Paxil, 80
People (magazine), 14, 24
Peurifoy, Reneau Z., 22
Pham, Kristina, 30
phobia(s)
age of onset, 38
causes of, 6, 11–12
definition of, 6
gender differences in, 38
impacts on health care, 72 (chart)
inheritance of, 42–43, 49
origin of term, 10
physical reactions to, 73 (illustration)
physiological explanations for, 13
prevalence of, 6
by type, 25 (chart)
seeking help for, 76–77
traumatic events and, 61–62
Phobias: Fighting the Fear (Saul), 38, 49, 68
Pitman, Roger, 45
Poe's Heart and the Mountain Climber (Restak), 9, 74
Popular Science (magazine), 49
post-traumatic stress disorder, 20

prefrontal cortex, 41, 50 (illustration), 52–53
Prevention (magazine), 68, 88
public speaking. fear of. *See* glossophobia

rain, fear of. *See* ombrophobia
Ratner, Jean, 76
Rauch, Scott, 81
Raynor, Rosalie, 40, 43, 44
Restak, Richard, 9, 25, 42, 45, 65, 74
Richards, Craig, 85
Rodino, Ellen, 67
Ross, Jerilyn, 63, 75, 77, 83
Ruddick, Julia, 19

San Francisco Chronicle (newspaper), 36
San Jose Mercury News (newspaper), 80
Saul, Helen, 38, 43, 47, 49, 64, 68
Saylor, Keith, 83
scelerophobia (fear of intruders), 36
Schuh, Dwight, 87
Segnit, Seymour, 65
separation anxiety disorder, 24
    among college freshman, symptoms of, 34 (chart)
serotonin, 42, 47, 53
Sevigny, Chloe, 29
Shawn, Allan, 8, 12, 25–26, 45, 46, 47, 64, 85
sick days, number taken, by mental illness, 69 (chart)
Silverman, Wendy, 84
snakes, fear of. *See* ophidiophobia
Snakes on a Plane (film), 32
social phobias, 6, 9–10, 65
    affects of, 55–56
    age of onset, 32, 68–69
    circumscribed, 22
    cognitive-behavioral therapy with antidepressants for, 91
    damaged to hippocampus from, 54
    economic impact of, 56–57

generalized, 23
inheritance of, 74
prevalence of, 38, 69
quality of life and, 16
reduced opportunities for sufferers of, 70 (chart)
suicide and, 68
symptoms of, 7
stage fright, 22
strangers, fear of. *See* xenophobia
stress, anxiety disorders and, 19
suicide
    social phobia and, 58, 68
    social phobias and, 71 (chart)

Teen People (magazine), 23
Thornton, Billy Bob, 27
Thurman, Uma, 30
Time (magazine), 49, 50, 55, 78, 79, 93
tissue plasminogen activator, 54
treatments, 16–17

uranophobia (fear of the heavens), 76
U.S. News and World Report (magazine), 15, 17, 41

virtual reality therapy, 18, 78–79, 83, 87
    for arachnophobia, 88, 89 (illustration)
vomiting, fear of. *See* emetophobia

Warhol, Andy, 55, 59–62
Watson, John B., 40, 43, 44
weather, fear of, 32
Wilson, Woodrow, 36
Wish I Could Be There: Notes from a Phobic Life (Shawn), 12, 25–26
women
    percent of phobia sufferers as, 50
    psychological factors in phobias in, 41

xenophobia (fear of strangers/ foreigners), 36

About the Author

Hal Marcovitz, a writer based in Chalfont, Pennsylvania, has written more than 100 books for young adult readers. His other titles in the Compact Research series include *Hepatitis* and *Meningitis*.